Doctrinal backgrounds of *Vipassanā*-meditation

Insight in current methods and according to canonical sources

BY

R.C. van Oosterwijk

Barkhuis
Groningen 2014

Book design: Barkhuis
Cover design: Mihnea Trusca

ISBN: 9789491431098

Table of contents

PART I

Chapter 1
Introduction

1.1 Meanings and popularity of *vipassanā*-meditation

The literal meaning of *vipassanā* is inward vision, insight, intuition and introspection.[1] It is a canonical term, as indexes to Pali editions of collections of discourses show. However, the connotations and canonical sources of the concept of *vipassanā*-meditation are not immediately clear. For instance *vipassanā* is different from right *sati* (mindfulness etc.) for which the method has been elaborated in the (*Mahā-*) *Satipaṭṭhāna-Sutta* (DN 22 and MN 10), and from right concentration as explained in many *sutta*s such as the *Sāmaññaphala-Sutta* (DN 2).[2]

Some teachers such as Sharon Salzberg even seem to use *vipassanā* as synonymous with mindfulness, although the latter concept is a translation of *sati* with associations to a modern psychological method. According to Tse-fu Kuan (2008: 10-1), 'The practice of mindfulness is widely considered to be the core of insight meditation by practitioners and scholars alike. However, there seems to have been no work that explains how mindfulness relates to insight meditation according to the earliest Buddhist texts.' Tse-fu Kuan tries to provide that relationship between *sati* and *vipassanā.* We intend to use the term 'mindfulness' only if a teacher we discuss uses it, or if *sati* is part of a process.

The focus of our research is on the doctrinal sources of *vipassanā*- practices. For convenience *vipassanā* will be translated into "insight". In the first part we will use '*vipassanā*-meditation' for all methods and practices aimed at reaching insight.

Vipassanā-meditation has become popular in South East Asia and the West. In Burma many lay people practice it. According to I. Jordt (2007: 205), it is a 'mass lay meditation movement.' The current methods and interpretations mostly follow recent teachers, as Sharf 1995 and Cousins showed.[3] According to Cousins (1996: 41), 'On the whole it seems that it

---

1 *Pali-English Dictionary,* PTS, London 1999 (1921).

2 See for other examples of right concentration *sutta*s DN 11, DN 12, DN 22; MN 4, MN 141, AN 3.88, and SN XLV,I,I, viii-V, 9.

3 Sharf, R.H. 1995: 242; Cousins, L. 1996.

is not possible, at present, to trace the lineage of the present day insight meditation tradition beyond the nineteenth century (in Burma).' Those recent teachers often offer different methods.[4]

The debate on the above issues is not only carried on among those teachers, but in the scientific community as well. Scholars such as Soma Thera, L. Schmithausen, Tilmann Vetter, Richard Shankman, and Bhikkhu Sujato have published about forms and sources of Theravāda Buddhist meditation.[5] Therefore our study fits in a discourse that is pursued by several scholars specialised in Buddhism and meditation.

1.2 Goal and questions for research

The goal of this research is to get a clearer picture of the doctrinal foundations of *vipassanā*-meditation, both according to the Pali canonical texts and to available translations from Chinese Buddhist sources in the *Āgamas*. This goal leads to the following questions for research. Which interpretations and sources of *vipassanā*-meditation (or '*vipassanā*-practice', *-bhāvanā* or '-contemplation') are used by recent and contemporary teachers? It seems interesting to analyse a wide range of such teachings. Which descriptions of the concept of *vipassanā*-meditation are offered in the Pali-*sutta*s (discourses)? For both categories, teachers and *sutta*s, we look at the following aspects of the process. How is the method of meditation explained? We will also mention if a teacher includes virtue in the method. Which insight is meant? What role is attributed to concentration or calmness? Which is the final step to awakening in these sources? Which differences between the concepts and methods of the teachers and the *sutta*s can be observed? Which approaches are widely accepted in the *sutta*s?

For the last point, the following criteria are chosen: a method or requirement is explained at least in *sutta*s of two Pali *Nikāya*s (collections), or in one *Nikāya* and the Pali *Vinaya*. Different collections were remembered by different groups of reciters. 'Since different *Nikāyas* were transmitted, and probably redacted, by different *bhāṇaka*s who were not influenced by the traditions of the *bhāṇaka*s of other *Nikāya*s,' ideas concerning the four *satipaṭṭhāna*s that occur in different *Nikāya*s are most likely to be early (Tse-fu Kuan 2008: 112). We generalize that idea for other important

[4] Bannaruji, B. (ed.), ca. 2006, *The five meditation techniques of Thai Buddhism*.
[5] Soma Thera 1971, Schmithausen 1981, Vetter 1988, Shankman 2008.

teachings. So, our criteria may lead to widely accepted and more or less independently transmitted renderings.

We will test these results by comparing them with *Āgama-sūtras*, as far as translated from Chinese redactions into English. The *Āgamas* are collections of canonical *sūtras* (discourses) of old Buddhist schools other than the Theravāda. The latter school has ordered the discourses in the *Nikāyas* of the Pali canon. The research will either show the variety of methods to develop insight or bring us closer to the essences. We will also mention *suttas* that offer the most complete training methods to insight.

1.3 Plan of this book

Part I

Chapter 1 introduces the controversies and the relevance of research on the doctrinal backgrounds of *vipassanā*-meditation. The purpose of this study is to obtain a clearer picture of the canonical foundations of *vipassanā*-meditation. This has led to a number of research questions on that subject.

Chapter 2 deals with the concept of *vipassanā*-meditation. In this chapter we describe a range of interpretations of *vipassanā*-meditation, the methods used and the canonical sources for these renderings. First we survey the teachings of recent and current teachers of *vipassanā*-meditation, and then those of some scholar-monks with a more analytical approach. However, we do not claim to be exhaustive in our treatment of teachers and authors. There are too many sources to make that feasible.

Chapter 3 is called recent teachings about *vipassanā*-meditation compared with Pali *suttas*. Here we discuss the methods presented in Chapter 2 on the basis of references to *suttas* and other Pali sources offered by the authors, or in relation to canonical texts which seem at first sight implied. It will become clear that calling the systematic training to develop insight towards wisdom "*vipassanā-bhāvanā*", should be preferred to *vipassanā*-meditation because the method may include thinking, analysis, contemplation, meditation, and other training practices. In part II we will apply this idea, translated as development of insight.

Part II

Chapter 4 deals with insight and its development according to *sutta*s in the *Vinaya*- and *Sutta-Piṭaka*. Here we switch the focus from the teachers and scholar-monks to the canonical sources, in particular the *sutta*s and a few famous teachings in the *Vinaya*. Which *sutta*s offer methods for development of *vipassanā*? *Sutta*s will be selected on the basis of references in the previous chapters, and indexes to the four main *Nikāya*s. As insight and wisdom (*paññā*) are both related to liberation by mental development and sometimes used as synonyms, we will also discuss "*paññāvimutti*". As a check we searched the internet-site www.accesstoinsight.org for the subject 'vipassana'. At the end of this chapter, a conclusion on the concept of *vipassanā-bhāvanā* in Pali canonical sources will be suggested. In this conclusion we discuss, which principles related to insight and practice to develop insight are widely accepted in the Pali *sutta*s, in particular by different traditions of reciters. Finally we suggest which Pali *sutta*s offer more or less complete methods to reach enlightenment including these principles, and which *sutta*s can complement the aspects missing.

Chapter 5 The development of insight in some *Āgama-sūtra*s will be compared with the Pali texts. This is intended as a first attempt to test the results of the analysis of Pali renderings in the previous chapters. We suppose that geographical distance limits late cross influences.

Chapter 6 Summary and conclusions

The results of this study on current methods of *vipassanā*-meditation, and requirements of systematic training to develop insight will be summarized in this chapter. Then we conclude which of the Pali discourses are most relevant for training towards insight. Furthermore, the conclusions from the comparison of some Chinese and Pali discourses in Chapter 5 will be drawn, followed by the final conclusions from the research.

Finally, references, abbreviations, a glossary of Pali and Sanskrit terms and an index of teachers and scholar-monks are included.

In quotations we use the spelling and diacritics as used by the author quoted. In our own text we will try to use the current conventions.

We would like to thank Bhikkhu Pāsādika (Prof. Bangert) and Katinka Hesselink, who made useful comments on an earlier draft.

Chapter 2

Interpretations of *vipassanā*-meditation

This chapter intends to show the current range of interpretations of *vipassanā*-meditation, the practices and the canonical sources for these renderings. The process of each practice is followed as far as possible.

2.1 Current ideas of teachers about the concept of *vipassanā*-meditation

How do recent and current teachers describe the concept of *vipassanā*-meditation? We analyze which method they use by following the process as taught, the insight to be gained and the final step to awakening. What role does each teacher attribute to concentration? Which canonical sources do they mention or seem to be implied? The teachings of teachers from the 19th century till the present have been ordered according to the most relevant *sutta* or other source they base themselves on.

2.1.1 Ajahn Chah

Venerable Ajahn Chah (1918-1993), who was the abbot of a Thai forest monastery, described first insight meditation (the practice of *vipassanā*) and then the practice of calming the mind (*samatha* meditation) in one of his teachings. Ajahn Chah explains the process of insight meditation as follows: if there is mindfulness there will be clear comprehension, and in general wisdom will arise.[6] 'However, we must constantly develop this wisdom through the practice of Insight Meditation' (Ajahn Chah 1982: 90).

This implies that we must see according to impermanence (*anicca*) as the basis, 'unsatisfactoriness' (*dukkha*), and no individual entity (*anattā*) (Ajahn Chah 1982: 91). We simply see that happy or sad states of mind are not permanent. 'We see they are unsatisfactory and that they aren't a

[6] Mindfulness has an important role: 'Just be mindful of what is. Our whole meditation is looking directly at the mind. You will see suffering, its cause and its end.' Interview with Ajahn Chah by J. Kornfield 1977: 48.

permanent self. If we continue to develop our mind in this way, we call it the practice of *Vipassanā* or Insight Meditation.' (Ajahn Chah 1982: 93) So we develop wisdom (*paññā*).

In another teaching Ajahn Chah is especially concentrating on *samādhi*. '*Samādhi* performs the function of calming or tranquilizing.' (Ajahn Chah 1991: 20)[7] 'Once the mind is calmed, then through the presence of *paññā* and the power of *samādhi* there will be increased composure and restraint. Energy is gained from the greater composure and refinement of mind and that energy helps to make *sīla* purer. This in turn helps give rise to *samādhi*, improves the quality of that *samādhi* which already exists and the development of *samādhi* facilitates and supports *paññā*.' (Ajahn Chah 1991: 20) Thus these three work together forming one whole, which provides the energy that gives rise to *vipassanā* (insight knowledge). *Sati* has to be continuously maintained, whatever you do (Ajahn Chah 1991: 20-1).

According to an interview with Ajahn Chah, *sīla* or discipline and morality are essential to support our practice; the intention is the main aspect (in Jack Kornfield 1977: 38). For his practice 'absorption is not necessary. You must establish a modicum of tranquillity and one-pointedness of mind. Then use this to examine yourself.' (In Kornfield 1977: 42) The practice of *samatha* by attention on the in-and-out-breath leads to calm, at that stage the mind will be clear and bright (Ajahn Chah 1982: 97-99). Then peace and happiness will arise.

To avoid attachment to this peace and happiness, we should contemplate that happiness is uncertain. We understand that the feeling of unhappiness is not lasting either. We see these things as natural, because there is wisdom. When we see everything as impermanent, this leads to a condition without anger or lust. We don't identify with or cling to what we like and dislike, because these cause suffering. 'Hence we understand that the Buddha's Teaching is to know suffering and to know what causes it to arise.' (Ajahn Chah 1982: 100) When we have the right understanding regarding these things and clearly understand freedom from suffering and the Path leading out of suffering, we see *Sacca Dhamma*. Practice leads to giving up all attachment. 'For Ajahn Chah enlightenment was attained by letting go.'[8] In brief, we suffer because we ascribe value to things, and

[7] A talk given in 1979 published in 1991. *Samatha* is a quiet mind while holding on to a meditation object; it is a 'samādhi-base' (Ajahn-Chah 1991: 27).

[8] Interview with J. Kornfield, a pupil of Ajahn Chah, in R. Shankman 2008: 109. See also Ajahn Chah 1982: 89.

because we are clinging to our various likes and dislikes. Ajahn Chah connected these ideas with knowing the four noble Truths.

Ajahn Chah (1982: 15, 20) taught that the practice of mindfulness of breathing ('Anapanasati') is a course for the development of morality, concentration and wisdom. This seems to be a reference to a canonical source.

2.1.2 Mettavīhari

Venerable Mettavīhari (1944-2007) was a Theravāda monk who taught *vipassanā*-meditation in the Netherlands. *Vipassanā* means insight into the real essence of existence (Mettavīhari 1989: III). We may see this as the concept of *vipassanā*, and the next point describes the core of the practice. 'The full time observation of yourself is true Vipassanā practice.' (Mettavīhari 1987: 9)

During a retreat, the four foundations of mindfulness should be observed or contemplated. Mettavīhari (1989: 1-3) explains several exercises for '*vipassanā*-meditation': sitting, going, standing, bowing and laying down.

Mettavīhari's practice stresses the importance of the sixteen *ñāṇa*s and follows their order. 'It is most important for one who practices Vipassanā to understand clearly the sixteen ñāṇas in successive order.' This is the first sentence in his book called *The sixteen ñāṇas* (1987). The 3rd *ñāṇa* is the knowledge of the 'universal characteristics': *anicca, dukkha, anattā*. According to Mettavīhari (1987: 23-4), in the 12th *ñāṇa* you realize the ultimate meaning of *vipassanā*-meditation. That 'marks the end of Vipassanā ñāṇa. There is nothing to be done further.' Mettavīhari connects this system of knowledge with the seven stages of purification, in which the sixth is the purity of insight-knowledge of the Path (*patipadā-ñāṇadassana-visudhi*) consisting of the progress from the 4th to the 12th *vipassanā ñāṇa*. Beyond the 12th *ñāṇa* progress depends on the *merit* earned in former lives. In the 14th *ñāṇa* it becomes easy to see the passing away of *nāma-rūpa* without worldly consciousness. The 15th *ñāṇa* constitutes the result (*Phala-ñāṇa*) and the 16th considers what has been realised (Mettavīhari 1987: 24-27).

2.1.3 Luangpor Teaan

The teaching of Luangpor Teaan (1911-1988) has been called dynamic meditation, which aims at liberating knowledge. The movement of the body is used to develop awareness (*sati*) of body and thoughts. A specific movement consists of moving the hands rhythmically up and down while sitting with the eyes open. However, awareness can be developed during all daily activities. 'Developing awareness only will lead you to achieve liberating knowledge (Paññā) from a clean, calm and clear mind. Paññā will release you from suffering, defilement, craving and attachment. Avijja will be replaced by Sati-Paññā.' (Bannaruji, B. 2006: 70-1)

Dynamic meditation is related to each of the four foundations of mindfulness. In the first foundation, one should become aware of each movement of the body. Having total awareness of body and mind, equanimity of feelings arises in the second foundation and then in the third one can see the arising of each thought. There seems to be a rank order in these, since the fourth can bring enlightenment, the release from suffering.

According to Luangpor Teaan, in the 4th foundation of mindfulness, which implies 'total awareness of body and mind, one will achieve steadiness of mind (Samathi). Paññā will arise in this state of mind. One can be released from suffering by Paññā, as one understands the law of nature. This is *Dhammanupassana*' (Bannaruji 2006: 73). One then sees the source of thought, which is the cause of suffering. There is a series of experiences that indicate progress for the practitioners. In that series the highest state is 'arising-extinguishing of the mind'.

2.1.4 Venerable Hiran

Venerable Hiran (Wat Sai Ngam, Thailand) teaches that the distinction between *vipassanā*-meditation and *satipaṭṭhāna*-meditation depends on the purpose. If the purpose is to see everything that happens inside, it is *vipassanā*. *Sīla* is important as a basis. The next step is to concentrate on the dominant feeling in the body. If you study the pain, you will note that nothing lasts long. In this way you come to see *anicca, dukkha* and *anattā*.[9] Hiran refers to the *Mahāsatipaṭṭhāna-Sutta* (DN 22) as the framework for his approach.

[9] Oral communication, December 2008-January 2009 at Wat Sai Ngam.

2.1.5 Achaan Naeb

Achaan Naeb (1897-1983) served as the head teacher at Boonkanjanaram meditation centre in Thailand. Boonkanjanaram offers theoretical background material in '*Vipassanā Bhavana*', which the editor translates as mind development through insight. According to Achaan Naeb 'In brief, insight is wisdom which enables one to see that mental states and matter are impermanent or transitory, unsatisfactory or suffering and impersonal or non-self.'[10]

Theory is important to cultivate the right method: 'she emphasizes that right conceptual understanding is necessary before practice.' (Kornfield 1977: 132) Momentary concentration (*kanika Samādhi*) is the basic tool to make *vipassanā pañña* work (*Vipassanā Bhavana* 1988: 31). The insight results from the practice of awareness as outlined in the *Mahāsatipaṭṭhāna-Sutta* (DN22). Their book also mentions the *Kāyānupassanā-Satipaṭṭhāna.* Following this practice leads to the first of the sixteen types of wisdom (*ñaṇās*). *Vipassanā paññā* is the type of wisdom that knows that there is only *rūpa* and *nāma,* and that they are impermanent, suffering and without self (*Vipassanā Bhavana* 1988: 30-1). When one sees this, there is a strong desire to end suffering.

The sixteen *ñāṇa*s are divided into three groups, of which numbers 4 to 12 are interpreted as *vipassanā-ñāṇa.* The wisdom of the 11th *ñāṇa* causes equanimity towards *rūpa* and *nāma*. There is neither dislike nor like of the mental and physical formations, but this equanimity is mixed with disgust. It is a strong wisdom and can get rid of most *kilesa* (unwholesome roots), because it sees *anicca, dukkha* and *anattā* very clearly. This is the highest *vipassanā* wisdom in the mundane sphere (*Vipassanā Bhavana* 1988: 95-6). However, the same is said about the 12th *ñaṇā* in which *dukkha-sacca* and *samudaya-sacca* are realized. *Magga-ñaṇā*, the 14th *ñaṇā* implies right understanding (*sammā-diṭṭhi*) of the four noble Truths. The power of the first *magga-citta* in this *ñaṇā* completely destroys the three unwholesome roots or defilements (*kilesa*: greed-*lobha,* anger-*dohsa* and bewilderment-*moha*). This first *magga-citta* is called *Sotāpatti-magga* (stream winner), but the three higher stages with *Arahatta-magga* as the highest are also included in *Magga-ñāṇa*. In the seven purities this 14th *ñāṇa* and the 15th are called purity of knowledge and vision (*ñaṇādassanavisuddhi*). The 15th *ñāṇa* constitutes the result (*Phala-ñāṇa*) and the 16th considers what has been realised.

---

[10] Achaan Naeb in Kornfield 1977: 134.

The practice taught in Boonkanjanaram consists of looking as a spectator at the suffering of the body, caused by any position. The effect of the pain is that we move to ease the discomfort (Kornfield 1977: 132). This process of changing mental states has to be closely watched, to develop wisdom through personal experience. Concentration brings no understanding of reality, it leads only to tranquillity and clinging.[11] Mixing concentration and insight does not lead to *vipassanā* wisdom, because *vipassanā*-meditation must have the changing of mental states and matter as its object.

2.1.6 Dhiravamsa

According to V.R. Dhiravamsa (born in 1934), who trained a long time as a monk in Thailand, *Vipassanā* is insight meditation. He explains meditation as 'the constant application of mindful awareness of whatever arises at the moment.' (Dhiravamsa 1990: 54) He sees this also as the essence of what the Buddha taught: 'The essence of his teaching lies in the truth of development and evolution of consciousness through the most effective tool--meditation.' (Dhiravamsa 1990: 158)

The instruction for the practice of insight meditation is 'to be constantly aware and mindful of whatever is arising in or entering the consciousness and body, knowing them for what they are without conceptualizing, labelling, or analyzing things into categories.' (Dhiravamsa 1990: 178) The starting object for meditation is the movement up and down of the belly with the breath (Dhiravamsa 1979: 33, 238). Look at feelings with bare attention, without judging, repressing or modifying anything. It is a process of discovering what is arising; especially fear of what might happen, and accepting it as it unfolds. This is basic to insight.

The domain of *vipassanā*-meditation consists of five factors: exertion of energy into the present moment; clarity of consciousness refers to clear seeing what is happening at the present moment; choiceless and desireless awareness is the key to move toward awakening; next is letting go of what is pleasurable, including the familiar self image or attempts to change people (non-doing what is harmful); maintaining an attitude of non-attachment to experiences and possessions (Dhiravamsa 1990: 180-8). The most subtle form of attachment is to the illusion of a separate-self. This prevents unity with the whole and other people. According to Dhiravamsa (1990: 184) impeccable, full awareness in every moment of living may be 'enlightenment'.

---

[11] Achaan Naeb in Kornfield 1977: 134, 141 and 155.

Insight meditation by means of the way of the *Satipaṭṭhāna*-Sutta leads to destruction of suffering and attainment of *Nibbāna*. Dhiravamsa (1990: 196-7) quotes both the beginning and the refrain of this discourse. In an older book, Dhiravamsa explains the foundations of *vipassanā*-meditation by offering a summary of the *Mahāsatipaṭṭhāna-Sutta* (Dhiravamsa 1979: 237-255). When awareness becomes part and parcel of life, insightful knowledge of the true nature of things arises. Hence, the process of arising and passing away becomes so obvious that the nature of impermanence and interdependence of things are clear to our mind, our intellect, and our consciousness. 'Thus arises the recognition and acknowledgement of the three characteristics of existence, namely, *impermanence, dissatisfactory nature*, and *voidness*.' (Dhiravamsa 1990: 197) Direct perception and insight into these characteristics destroys the idea of an eternal self.

Dukkha has not been treated in Dhiravamsa's description of *vipassanā*-meditation. However, Dhiravamsa (1990: 92) explains the contemplative perception of *dukkha* as welcoming and accepting it when it arises or comes to us. The 'fourth floor of enlightenment' is called 'Arahantship', this brings the destruction of clinging to any *jhāna* state, of I-conceit, restlessness and ignorance, the latter being absence of insight (Dhiravamsa 1990: 161).

Concentration meditation is apt to produce psychosomatic disturbances; it may lead to knowledge and power, but not to insight (Dhiravamsa 1990: 179-80). His reason is that insight cannot be produced. We will come back to this point in paragraph 3.1.6.

2.1.7 Flickstein

According to M. Flickstein (2003: 165), the goal of insight meditation is to see the things as they really are. We understand his method as follows: purification of discipline is developed by following the rules for ethical behaviour. Mindfulness of in-and-out breathing purifies consciousness. When we are not aware of the breath anymore, but note it again with a little more effort and sense a glaring light, stars or a clear disk, together with a happy feeling, then we have reached access concentration.

Now we can start insight meditation, or go on with *jhāna*. Access concentration is sufficient to calm the mind and suppress the hindrances temporarily (Flickstein 2003: 70). However, on p. 81 Flickstein states that momentary concentration is sufficient as well. According to Flickstein (2003:

71), 'contemplation' refers to mindfulness and insight meditation instead of cognitive reflection.[12]

The practice to start with is attention directed at the body as a body, to recognise that the body is impermanent, or not mine, or unsatisfactory. If we experience one of these characteristics of existence we have reached clear understanding of the body. The process continues with exercises for feelings. We work during one day with one of the sense faculties, noting that feelings (pleasant to unpleasant) arise when there is contact with that faculty. Another exercise for feelings is pain as an object of attention.

The next step is mindfulness of the mind. During attention on the breath, we categorize thoughts as 'desire'; or 'hatred' including fear of the future; or 'confusion' such as doubt of the usefulness of meditation or a restless mind. On the other hand we recognise a calm mind, or loving kindness, as 'wisdom' (Flickstein 2003: 118-9). During a second exercise one experiences the mind as impermanent, unsatisfactory and not self. To be mindful of '*dhamma*s' means here: mindfulness of everything that exists, such as the five elements of existence (*khandha*),[13] the seven factors of enlightenment, and finally the four noble Truths. To banish desire ends suffering and one reaches the third Truth (Flickstein 2003: 148).

The Path starts with 'right view' as intellectual, conceptual understanding of the four noble Truths. The final step is an intuitive and direct awareness of the meaning of these Truths (Flickstein 2003: 149-50). According to Flickstein (2003:164), purification by knowledge and insight regarding the Path is the last stage before *Nibbāna*, but 'purification by knowledge and insight' comes next and leads to the supramundane states. When we practice insight meditation long enough, we will experience the 16 stages of intuitive insight (Flickstein 2003: 87-8).

Flickstein (2003: 21) refers to several sources for his method. He uses the seven stages of purification of the *Rathavinīta-Sutta* (MN 24). He notes that these stages have not been elaborated in the canon, but only in the *Visuddhimagga*. He correlates these stages with the exercises of DN 22 in his method, admitting this has no foundation in the canon (Flickstein 2003: 23).

---

[12] The Dutch translator notes that this differs from DN 22.

[13] Here the translation by K.R. Norman (1989 (1971): 181-2) of *khandha* as 'element of existence' is followed, since it is acceptable to T. Vetter (2000: 317) as well. Other translations: constituents, aggregates.

2.1.8 Christina Feldman

Christina Feldman describes *vipassanā* practice, or the insight path, as 'an inclusive practice that embraces all the foundations of mindfulness.'[14] Feldman has been teaching meditation since 1974 (Shankman 2008: 155). The meditator must be in touch with changing experiences to gain insight into the impermanence, the selfless nature, and the suffering character of these experiences (in Shankman 2008: 148). According to Feldman (in Shankman 2008: 153), *jhāna* is not mentioned much in the *Satipaṭṭhāna-Sutta*. The *Ānāpānasati-Sutta* (MN 118) can be taught as an insight practice or as a *samatha* practice, perhaps depending on the intention (in Shankman 2008: 154).

One-pointedness with whatever object arises is the kind of *samādhi* that is very important to the development of insight. Feldman agrees this is a momentary concentration (Shankman 2008: 146-7). Often people do not have enough concentration for insight to penetrate. Therefore, Feldman develops *samatha* and *vipassanā* together. However, liberating insight is possible without strong *samādhi*. Insight practice is also possible if one forms the intention to obtain insight in the changing experiences, before getting into access concentration or into the first *jhāna*. Within deeper states of absorption the mind is too calm to have insight in changing experiences.

2.1.9 Mahāsi Sayādaw

Mahāsi Sayādaw (1904-1982) was a Burmese monk, who had an impact on the teaching of *vipassanā*-meditation in Thailand and the West.[15] The preliminary steps are giving up worldly thoughts and actions during training for purification of conduct, and observe at least the eight rules of discipline. 'His style of meditation involved quietly noting the rising and falling of the abdomen during breathing.' (Bannaruji 2006: 45) In this exercise, 'noting' means mentally naming 'rising' and 'falling' (Bannaruji 2006: 46). Then one has to note any thought, intention or feeling that arises and any activity. If pain 'becomes almost unbearable, you must ignore the pain' (Mahāsi 1977: 59). By day and night (when not asleep) practicing

---

[14] Interview with Feldman in Shankman 2008: 146.

[15] Mahāsī was the most influential teacher in Burma around 1950 as well. His *satipaṭṭhāna* method is traced back to the Thilon Sayādaw, a forest monk of the time of king Mindon (G. Houtman 1999: 8).

this method and walking meditation, the insight of the practitioner will gradually grow.

The higher stages of insight are: 'to see rising-extinction of *nāma* and *rūpa*, impermanence of *nāma* and *rūpa* (*aniccānupassana ñāṇa*), non-self of *nāma* and *rūpa* (*anattānupassana ñāṇa*), and detachment from the five Elements of existence or *nāma* and *rūpa*. Constantly practising, the mind realises what defilements are eradicated. A noble one can be expected to emerge.' (Bannaruji 2006: 49). The impermanence of *nāma* and *rūpa* means that the meditator will see for himself that whatever arises will disintegrate within a short period of time. This universal impermanence is terrible, fearful and unsatisfactory (Mahāsi 1977: 71, 76-7).

Elsewhere Mahāsi Sayādaw calls the next stages after seeing impermanence thus: "*dukkhānupassana ñāṇa*" and then "*anattānu-passana ñāṇa*" (Mahāsi Sayādaw, transl. 1989 (1979): 23). The knowledge about impermanence leads to the understanding that the impermanence of the body-and-mind process is unsatisfactory, the suffering applies as well to problems of the body. To realise that all these psycho-physical factors arise out of themselves and are independent of the will constitutes the knowledge of the non-self of *nāma* and *rūpa*. The steadfast insight without any reflection that all these five elements of existence are *anicca*, *dukkha* and *anattā* leads to equanimity about formations (Mahāsi 1977: 78-9). 'As soon as faith, energy, mindfulness, concentration, and wisdom are developed in an even manner, he will realize nirvana.' (Mahāsi 1977: 80)

In other literature on Mahāsi Sayādaw's method good concentration (*samādhi*) is briefly mentioned. If concentration cannot develop, it cannot result in insight (Mahāsi Sayādaw, transl. 1979 (1989): 11). Kornfield, who studied also with Mahāsi, notes: 'For Mahāsi Sayādaw the way to enlightenment was through the progress of insight and very deep, sustained, profound mindfulness and concentration.'[16] However, in an earlier book Kornfield (1977: 52) wrote about Mahāsi's method: 'Mahāsi's approach to mindfulness is developed strictly as an insight practice from the first. There is no special preparatory development of concentration on one object. Instead, from the very beginning, one establishes awareness of the moment-to-moment change of body and mind.'

According to G. Houtman (1999: 308), Mahāsi's tradition is a 'dry'-visioned *vipassanā* method, worried about the worldly implications of *samatha*. This would imply that he considers momentary concentration or access concentration to be sufficient for insight. However, Mahāsi seems

[16] Shankman (2008: 109) cites J. Kornfield from his interview with him.

to interpret momentary concentration different in different stages of purification. 'So he [Mahāsi] speaks of the stage of purification of mind being accomplished by momentary concentration which is similar in strength to access.' 'Likewise the highest stage of the sixth purification is by momentary concentration which has a strength equivalent to that of full absorption.' (L.S. Cousins 1996: 47-8)

According to Mahāsi (1977: 54-5), the right way for mind-training by contemplation is found in the *Mahāsatipaṭṭhāna-Sutta.*

Furthermore, Nyanaponika (1975 (1962): 87-107) offers interesting detailed instructions for Mahāsi's Burmese method of bare insight, that is without first attaining *jhāna.* There should be general mindfulness of the four postures during the day, and noticing all activities and feelings. Then one sits with one leg on the other or both legs on the ground. The gaze may rest on a geometrical object. The primary object is bare noticing of the rise and fall of the abdomen. If this remains unclear, one should turn the attention to perceptions of touching by parts of the body and sitting (Nyanaponika 1975 (1962): 95).

One should change posture if the pain persists, then the practice of mindful walking is recommended. One should be aware of breaks in attention, undesirable thoughts or distractions for example: 'mind with anger' or 'sound'. Then one should return to the interrupted meditation subject. It is desirable that a determined practice starts with a number of weeks exclusively devoted to it. Periods of three to four hours of continuous mindfulness are regarded as the minimum for a beginner undergoing a course of strict practice (Nyanaponika 1975 (1962): 98).

2.1.10 Buddhadasa Bhikkhu

The late Buddhadasa Bhikkhu (1906-1993) taught several meditation techniques for *vipassanā.* Among these attention to breathing is central, but in his system the breath is followed at the tip of the nose. This can lead to a level of concentration below meditative absorption (*jhāna*), from which level on *vipassanā* can be practiced.

Buddhadasa also taught the development of investigation of the breath while sitting for *vipassanā* (Bannaruji 2006: 57-9). To develop *vipassanā* the practitioners first learn awareness of breathing in and out, until they can follow the breath steadily and smoothly. Then they investigate and note the length of the breath. Furthermore they examine whether the breath is refined or unrefined. The next step investigates *rūpa* and *nāma*; in this case the first is the breath and the latter awareness (*sati*) that knows the breath flowing in and out.

Contemplation of the five elements of existence shows the reality of the practitioner's lives. They contemplate 'rising' and 'extinction' and realize that they consist of *rūpa* and *nāma*. Because of our lack of control of the five elements of existence these are impermanent and not as we wish. Therefore they are non-self, contemplate this. Continuous contemplating the fading away of the five elements of existence, attachment to them ceases. Then fading away, cessation and relinquishment of the defilements constitute the beginning of *nibbāna ñāṇa*, this knowledge helps the practitioner to attain *nibbāna*. A practitioner 'will become a noble one' (Bannaruji 2006: 61).

Buddhadasa explained a similar process of walking meditation for *vipassanā*. The above means to practice *vipassanā*, as the following sentence indicates. 'The practitioners continuously follow the above instructions in the "Vipassana Practice".' (Bannaruji 2006: 61)

2.1.11 Bhikkhu Gunaratana

Bhikkhu Gunaratana (ordained in 1947) considers 'to be attentive' as the core of *vipassanā*-meditation, as it is both the goal and the means of this meditation (H. Gunaratana 2008 (2002): 164). He prefers attention to the breath as the method. Each tetrad of the *Ānāpānasati Sutta* is complete in itself. At the end of each tetrad, even the first on mindfulness of the body, you can practice the seven factors of enlightenment.[17] We can only develop wisdom by being attentive, by observing everything that occurs in the mind. To be attentive means to look at everything that arises in the mind without categorizing. Just observe what is. One will note continuous change of thoughts, feelings, and emotions. It is all a process, not a self.

Cultivation of attentiveness and concentration need to be developed in a balanced way (Gunaratana 2008: 167). Access concentration is not strong enough to penetrate non self etc. at the deepest level (in Shankman 2008: 138). 'Only when you are in jhāna, not out of jhāna, can you see the most subtle reality in the body and mind' (in Shankman 2008: 141). On the same page Gunaratana also indicates the functions of mindfulness, concentration and equanimity. 'Equanimity is the balancing factor. Concentration is the sharpening factor. Mindfulness is the seeing factor. When

[17] Interview with Gunaratana in Shankman 2008: 141.

these three come together you can see reality exactly as it is'. During insight meditation there will arrive a moment in which one experiences the transience of existence, the unsatisfactoriness even to the extent that human life is suffering and selfless in a penetrative way. One awakes to the futility of greed, desire and defensiveness; the idea of a self dissolves (Gunaratana 2008: 196). What remains is peace, *Nibbāna*.

Gunaratana does not see the idea of dry insight, a concept that refers to acquiring insight without reaching concentration, in the *sutta*s. 'Dry insight, without the support of mental calm, is a commentarial idea. You can never find any reference to dry insight in the Sutta Piṭaka.' (In Shankman 2008: 136) So concentration is necessary. According to Gunaratana as quoted above, concentration reaching *jhāna* is needed to see reality. The joy and happiness trained in MN 118 are not *jhāna*; rather this *sutta* refers to ordinary joy and happiness (in Shankman 2008: 143).

2.1.12 Pa Auk Sayādaw

According to Pa Auk Sayādaw *vipassanā* practice means to penetrate again and again into ultimate materiality and see clearly.[18] Pa Auk was ordained in 1954. He accepts two ways to practice *vipassanā*-meditation.

First, he emphasizes mindfulness of breathing, *ānāpānasati*, to train systematically the awareness of the breath. Then *jhāna* has to be developed by means of certain signs of concentration. When the fourth *jhāna* has been reached, a strong powerful light called 'the light of wisdom' is produced. 'The fourth jhāna is the foundation for vipassanā.' (In Shankman 2008: 178) Then quickly switch your attention to the four-elements as the meditation object.[19] 'Upon emerging from the fourth jhāna, you shift to four-elements systematically, and at that time there is no jhāna and no access concentration. But there still is light.' (In Shankman 2008: 178) You will see the four (great) elements meditation and the *kalāpa*s, or small particles, because the fourth *jhāna* is subtle. Practice again and again and one will see clearly ultimate materiality and mentality.

[18] Interview with Pa Auk Sayadaw in Shankman 2008: 180.

[19] Here the four-elements remain undefined. According to MN 28 (I, 185), the four elements are earth, water, fire and air. The visible human body consists of these elements.

Secondly, the alternative Pa Auk offers is based on the *Visuddhimagga*: One can begin with the practice of four elements meditation systematically (in Shankman 2008: 178-9). When one sees *kalāpa*s, one has to analyze four elements in each *kalāpa*. This is a level of four elements concentration, called *vipassanā samādhi*, which is nearly the same as access concentration related to *ānāpāna*. In this way one can reach stream-entry without *jhāna*.

As *vipassanā* tires the mental body, there comes a moment you cannot see clearly anymore. Then you should go back to one of the *jhāna* attainments to rest, for this purpose he recommends the base of neither-perception-nor-nonperception (in Shankman 2008: 180). Pa Auk Sayādaw emphasizes mindfulness of breathing as a *samatha* meditation practice. According to Houtman (1999: 308), the Hpa Auk Sayādaw aims to scale the heights of both *samatha* and *vipassanā*.

2.1.13 Ledi Sayādaw

According to Ledi Sayādaw (1846-1923) three types of knowledge are relevant for insight in the three characteristics of existence or 'salient marks':

> '1. *Anicca-vipassanā-ñāṇa*: Insight knowledge in contemplating impermanence;
> 2. *dukkha-vipassanā-ñāṇa* Insight knowledge in contemplating ill and;
> 3. *anattā-vipassanā-ñāṇa*: Insight knowledge in contemplating no-soul.'
> (Ledi Sayādaw 1986 (1915): 70)

The first insight, impermanence, has to be discerned to acquire the third insight, no-soul. Ledi Sayādaw (1986 (1915): 71) cites a text addressed to Meghiya in support of this point.

Ledi Sayādaw (1986 (1915): 72) recommends the arising and ceasing of the four great elements and noting the changes of consciousness as the relevant exercises to develop insight. However, knowledge of *dukkha* remains incomplete, and so lust and conceit can only be destroyed during the four grades of the transcendental path (Ledi Sayādaw 1986 (1915): 70). Only insight knowledge leads to 'the eradication of defilements at the moment of attaining the paths (*magga*) of emancipation (*sotāpatti-magga*, etc.);' (Ledi Sayādaw 1986 (1915): 73). The fruition-stages of these paths result in the tranquilization of defilements. 'The knowledge pertaining to *arahatta-magga*, the fourth path, dispels the defilements which were left un-dispelled by the lower paths' (Ledi Sayādaw 1986 (1915): 76). Final escape from the defilements is reached on attaining *Nibbāna*.

The *jhānas* can temporarily dispel the mental defilements. However, these do not give long term results. According to G. Houtman (1999: 308), *vipassanā* methodologies arising from the *ānāpāna* tradition of the Ledi Sayādaw tend to involve identifiable *samatha* practice.

2.1.14 Acharn Mun

Acharn Mun (1870-1949) taught *samatha-vipassanā*, a practice combining calm and insight. First a meditator should be aware of breathing in and out, in the chest. At the same time use the word 'Bud' at breathing in and 'Dho' breathing out. One should practice all the time. When the practitioner reaches attainment concentration, he should use this *samatha* to contemplate the repulsive nature of the parts of the body (Bannaruji 2006: 40). This is *vipassanā* to uproot the defilements. A specific part of the body may appear as a mental image during meditation. This is a sign of attaining a concentration called access concentration (*upacāra samādhi*).

Then, the practitioner should separate the body into the elements earth, water, fire, and air until an image of the body, the mind and the entire world having one and the same inherent nature arises. This stage is called the clear insight that both knows and sees things for what they actually are ('*yathabhūtañāṇa-dassana vipassanā*'). Next the practitioner should analyse things as impermanent and suffering and investigate all things as non-self until the mind is made to converge. Then he can see truly the clear insight leading to emergence ('*vutthana-gamini vipassanā*'). 'At this stage there is a turning point of release that ends suffering' (Bannaruji 2006: 40-1).

2.1.15 Leigh Brasington

Leigh Brasington, a contemporary teacher, asserts: 'The Buddha first teaches the morality section and abandoning the hindrances, and then he teaches the jhānas, and finally the directing of the mind to knowledge and vision.'[20] Most *suttas* that go to enlightenment include the *jhānas* according to a standard formula. Brasington prefers to teach a graduated system

[20] Interview with Brasington in Shankman 2008: 160. He teaches meditation since 1997 (Shankman 2008: 165).

based on for example the *Sāmaññaphala-Sutta* (DN 2). According to this teacher, access concentration is required to suppress the hindrances, in particular hankering and grief for the world. Access concentration means unbroken mindfulness of the meditation object to Brasington.

When one comes in DN 2 to the part about directing the mind to knowledge and vision, one inserts the 21 *Satipaṭṭhāna-Sutta* practices (in Shankman 2008: 160). A deeper level of *samādhi* will make the insight practice of investigating body and mind more efficient. 'All of jhāna practice as well as access concentration is a warm-up exercise to the main event, which is insight practice.' (In Shankman 2008: 165) However, Brasington accepts that *jhāna* is difficult to reach, and that any amount of concentration as a preparation for insight is helpful (in Shankman 2008: 157).

Brasington does not believe in insight practice while in *jhāna*. He argues: 'That unification of mind that appears in the second jhāna, by definition, I would think, precludes doing any sort of investigation.' (In Shankman 2008: 164) Attachment to *jhāna* is no problem for insight practice, because the insight will be more interesting.

Brasington suggests that *ānāpānasati* forms one of the few teachings in the *sutta*s that goes all the way to enlightenment, without including the *jhāna*s. Steps one to four of this *sutta* lead to access concentration, which suppresses the hindrances. The last four steps of the *Ānāpānasati-Sutta* are insight practice (in Shankman 2008: 159-60). Steps five through twelve of *ānāpānasati* deepen the concentration beyond access. There *pīti* (joy) and *sukha* (happiness) are mentioned. However, these middle eight steps are not necessarily identical with the *jhāna*s (in Shankman 2008: 159-60).

2.1.16 Ajahn Thānissaro

Ajahn Thānissaro (ordained in 1976) offers a concise description of his system to reach insight, the role of concentration and the final step to awakening. He shows how to use the *jhāna*s to acquire insight thus: 'You can use any of the jhānas as a basis for awakening, from the first one up. In each case you analyze the jhāna in terms of the five elements of existence, which you come to see as stressful, not-self, impermanent, a dart, a cancer, an emptiness, and on down the line. In this way you develop a sense of dispassion and disenchantment for even the ease of jhāna. That's how you let go.'[21] Mastering *jhāna* makes calm and insight stronger.

---

[21] Interview with Ajahn Thānissaro in Shankman 2008: 123.

Thānissaro sees no clear line between a mindfulness practice, a concentration practice, and an insight practice. Besides he teaches that you need all of these. Thānissaro (in Shankman 2008: 123) interprets *vipassanā* as a quality of the mind, not something to do. You have to use any state of concentration for 'understanding stress and abandoning the cause of stress' (in Shankman 2008: 128). However, you need to pull back a little bit from a *jhāna*, particularly from the second one up, without losing that concentrated state.

According to Thānissaro, AN 4.126 (II, 130), AN 9.36 (IV, 422 ff.), MN 52, and MN 121 contain passages with people who can analyse a specific *jhāna* while they are in it. It will be interesting to see how these discourses explain this.

2.1.17 Candasaro Bhikkhu

Candasaro Bhikkhu (1884-1959) founded Vijja Dhammakāya, a path consisting of *samatha, anupassana* (constant observation) and *vipassanā* (Bannaruji 2006: 87). A teacher guides the students through the exercises. Concentration on a clear crystal ball can lead to the emergence of more and more refined forms. Constant observation should be practiced, until the mind reaches the wisdom through which a noble state is developed (*Dhammakāya-Gotrabhu*). It appears like a large diamond Buddha statue.

This 'is a basis for the development of *vipassanā* for enlightenment' (Bannaruji 2006: 88-9). A desire to release oneself from defilement arises. From that basis *Dhammakāya* spheres appear, looking like larger and larger diamond Buddha statues. From there on one should contemplate the four Noble Truths in refined human form and certain other divine forms. 'The practitioner will realize the Three Characteristics of Things through contemplating the spheres; namely, suffering, impermanence and non-self. Through such practices, they can eradicate ten fetters or binds (*Saṇyojana*) and become the *Arahanta* (the Perfect One)' (Bannaruji 2006: 89).

2.1.18 Jack Kornfield

As mentioned, Jack Kornfield was a student of both Ajahn Chah and Mahāsi Sayādaw. In some respects Kornfield developed their teachings. He has taught meditation since 1974 (Shankman 2008: 116). Insight meditation concentrates on changing objects to probe the mind-body process (Kornfield 1977: 11).

Mindfulness is the key to the practice of *vipassanā*-meditation. Kornfield (1977: 14) refers to one of the last instructions of the Buddha as "strive on with mindfulness". We return to this translation, supposedly of DN 16 (II, 156), in the next Chapter. Mindfulness is practiced by bare-attention, a seeing without reacting, to our world of experiences, to the body, feelings and to the changing objects of consciousness. With penetrating awareness of our own process we see more and more sharply how all things are changing, not offering a source of lasting happiness, and that the process is independent of a permanent self or a lasting soul.

These insights lead to wisdom, bringing equanimity and seeing the unity of all beings with compassion. 'When the mind is completely balanced, tranquil, and keenly alert, one may experience ... the peace of nirvāna' (Kornfield 1977: 12). Furthermore insight into emptiness, detachment and a mind free from defilements arise. Purity of mind is freedom from greed, hatred and delusion. 'Let go and all suffering will cease.' (Kornfield 1977: 31)

Kornfield (1977: 12) has once thought that only moment to moment concentration to changing objects was necessary. He seems to have changed his teaching into: it is skilful to practice both mindfulness and concentration, but without much striving. Kornfield advises to dwell in well being or other *jhāna* factors as they begin to arise. 'It [Wisdom] can grow deep later on, when concentration is turned toward wisdom.' (Kornfield in Shankman 2008: 111-113). Kornfield uses wisdom resolutions when coming out of *jhāna*, to deepen understanding, such as: 'May a deep insight into anicca arise.' (In Shankman 2008: 114)

2.1.19 Sharon Salzberg

Sharon Salzberg has led meditation retreats since 1974 (Shankman 2008: 135). According to Salzberg deep insight into impermanence, suffering and not self can be reached by mindfulness. "The ancient Buddhist practices of vipassana (mindfulness) and metta (loving-kindness) are the foundations of her work." (Front page of www.sharonsalzberg.com). So Salzberg seems to equate *vipassanā* and mindfulness.

Salzberg emphasises 'a moment-to-moment continuity of mindfulness.' She calls this 'A momentary concentration.'[22] This is according to Salzberg's experience sufficient for deep insight. '...I know it's true from experience and from seeing others, that momentary concentration and continuous mindfulness provide a platform for a deep insight into anicca, dukkha, and anattā, then you don't need that sort of specific devotion to jhāna.' (In Shankman 2008: 132) Knowing a sound without distortions, such as greed, in the mind is being mindful. Moment-to-moment awareness that is not distorted by grasping, aversion, or delusion constitutes a moment of liberation.

Some degree of a concentrated mind is important; however Salzberg discourages the development of the *jhāna* factors. According to Salzberg these lead to attachment, which is very painful (in Shankman 2008: 130). Although momentary concentration is deemed to be sufficient, access concentration is helpful as well. The latter may be developed by focussing on which object is predominant. The mind becomes still but the flow of experiences still happens.

2.1.20 U Ba Khin

U Ba Khin (1899-1971) was a Burmese lay meditation master. According to his teaching method, 'Vipassanā-meditation is concerned with mindfulness of the process of moment-to-moment change'.[23]

The noble eightfold path must be followed. First virtue is necessary, and next concentration on the incoming and outgoing breath must be developed. Concentration to one-pointedness is encouraged by focus of attention to a spot on the upper lip at the base of the nose, synchronizing the in and out breath with the awareness of these streams, called '*ānāpāna*' (In Kornfield 1977: 245).

When progress is made in concentration, flashes or points of light or a tiny star or moon or sun appear during meditation with closed eyes. Try to repeat this quickly after each short break. The best level of concentration is reached when you can keep the point of light stationary for some time, which is called access concentration. 'When you can do this, you are ready

[22] Interview with Salzberg in Shankman 2008: 130.

[23] U Ba Khin in Kornfield 1977: 251.

to be switched to Vipassanā-meditation to gain insight into the ultimate truth and enjoy the great peace of nirvāna' (U Ba Khin in Kornfield 1977: 246).

The third state of the noble eightfold path is wisdom or insight.[24] The characteristics of wisdom are right aspiration and right understanding. Now the focus of attention is switched to the inside. The meditator gets instruction on how to sweep the attention through the body, from head to feet and from feet to head to experiencc matter and sensations as change. By this introspection the meditator first makes an analytical study of matter and then of mind and mental properties. He begins to realize that these are built of minute particles (*kalāpas*) that are in constant change. And thus matter and mind are impermanent and fleeting.

If you know experience and understand the nature of impermanence, suffering and egolessness appear as well. The nature of the internal forces (the atoms in a state of perpetual friction, heat, cold and combustion) makes clear that the five elements of existence are suffering. The elimination of the negative forces or impurities within creates an upheaval that may create a sensation of burning, which should not persist.[25] As there is no unchanging substance, there is no substantiality in the so-called self. As the truth of suffering is realized, its causes become automatically destroyed.

The final stages of the *vipassanā* practice are thus: 'By continued practice the yogi then ceases to have any passion or anger. Eventually he experiences the full freedom of arahantship as the final goal.' (In Kornfield 1977: 247) U Ba Khin referred to the final words of the Buddha to stress the importance of impermanence: "Decay and impermanence is inherent in all compound things. Work out your own salvation with diligence." (In Kornfield 1977: 249) That refers to *sutta* DN 16.

2.1.21 Goenka

S.N. Goenka is known as a pupil of U Ba Khin (Kornfield 1977: 238). So, one would expect a very similar training method. Still there are differences in the method taught and the explanations. In Goenka's system *Vipassanā-bhāvanā* is a gradual training to develop insight, starting with practicing moral behaviour. Next one practices to observe bare respiration, without

---

[24] This ´third state´ of the Path refers to the summary version comprising morality, concentration, and wisdom.

[25] Summary of Kornfield's (1977: 237-8) quotes of U Ba Khin, without specified sources.

regulating it, or adding any word. Only observe, because the goal is purification of the mind, but not concentration (Goenka 1995: 11). The mind is kept on the breath at the nostrils (U Ba Khin: a spot on the upper lip at the base of the nose). The mind must be tamed and trained by continuous practice (Goenka 1995: 19). W. Hart has written *The art of living: as taught by S.N. Goenka*. According to Hart (1987: 116), keeping the awareness from moment to moment on breathing and as long as possible is right concentration.

Then the third section of the Path called wisdom or insight (*paññā*) must be practiced, which totally purifies the mind (Goenka 1995: 21). *Vipassanā-bhāvanā* is a step-by-step method to develop insight (Hart 1987: 136). The instruction for sweeping is more detailed than U Ba Khin's. Attention should be fixed on sections of the body, preferably two or three inches wide, until you feel a sensation. The sensation will be first outside and later inside. 'One must learn to be aware of different sensations without reacting to them, accepting their changing, impersonal nature' (Goenka 1995: 36). Awareness of sensations, and experiencing that they change, without reacting is equanimity. This teaches that sensations are bound to pass away (*anicca*). The changes of all processes in our body and mind also teach that there is no real, unchanging self (Hart 1987: 142). Examine pain that arises as if it were someone else's pain, again without reacting (Goenka 1995: 44).

Goenka explains the chain of dependent arising. One must understand that all suffering in life arises because of reactions to liking and disliking, leading to desire and aversion. *Saṅkhārā* are both the mental reactions to liking and disliking and the result of old mental reactions to such sensations. So the advice is to break the chain at the sensations by observing with equanimity and understanding 'this will also change' (Goenka 1995: 47-9). Then perceive with true insight 'all *saṅkhārā* are impermanent' (Goenka 1995: 51). This is the path of purification.

When we do not react, there is space in the psychical stream, and then an old reaction becomes apparent. If we do not react to that reaction either, the old conditioned reflex will disappear (Hart 1987: 163). When *saṅkhārā* are eradicated the happiness of freedom from misery arises (Goenka 1995: 69). One obtains insight in the own mind, with which we can recognise the causes of suffering and end these (Hart 1987: 131). Hart (1987: 131) refers to DN 16 "The mind imbued with wisdom becomes completely free from the corruptions".[26] He also refers to *Udāna* I.x and VIII.i.

[26] We used Walshe's (1987: 255) translation of DN 16 [123], as Hart wrote in Dutch.

2.2 Summary of the methods of teachers of *vipassanā*-meditation

The methods of *vipassanā*-meditation taught by these twenty-one teachers are diverse. However, there are also common aspects between many of these practices. Fifteen of the twenty-one teachers investigated, base their methods of *vipassanā*-meditation on a form of *sati*-practice as taught in *sutta*s DN 22, MN 10, 118 or 119. Two of these teachers use combinations of DN 22 with either DN 2 or MN 24. Furthermore, three teachers apply the analysis of the four great elements. Discourse MN 62 explains this method as well as attention to breathing. For three teachers we could not trace a *sutta* as a basis for their practice.

According to fifteen teachers *vipassanā* means, or *vipassanā* practice develops, the clear insight that body and mind are impermanent, suffering and non-self. Mettavīhari teaches that this understanding happens early in the process, in the 3rd *ñāṇa* of the 16 knowledges. Buddhadasa and Dhiravamsa have mentioned two of these so called characteristics or marks of existence. We did not trace these characteristics of existence as the insight to be developed in our sources about Luangpor Teaan, Pa Auk Sayādaw, and Brasington.

Some other terms used to describe *vipassanā* besides insight are: clear insight, deep insight, real knowledge and vision, understanding, seeing, intuitive insight, experiences and understands, realisation, see reality, insight knowledge, and liberating knowledge. These terms try to make clear that this knowledge must be experienced and understood. We might say that it has to be internalised.

The part of concentration in the development of insight varies according to the teachers. One teacher (Dhiravamsa) states that concentration has no role in the development of insight. Momentary concentration is sufficient according to three teachers, while three others think that access concentration (*upacara samādhi*) is necessary or at least best. Two teachers believe concentration should remain below the level of *jhāna.*

However, according to two other teachers you can see reality only during concentration at the level of *jhāna*, while two more estimate that one can reach insight only after coming out of *jhāna. Sutta*s AN 4.126 (II, 130), AN 9.36 (IV, 422 ff.), MN 52, and MN 121 are indicated as canonical sources to explain that insight during *jhāna* is possible. The approaches to describe the final step to awakening are too diverse to make a summary useful.

These findings lead to the first working hypothesis: Practices which only teach attention to the breath only teach one step of the eightfold Path, namely *sati*.

Second working hypothesis: a) The level of concentration needed to reach clear insight is not indicated in an unequivocal way in the *suttas*.
b) The idea that momentary concentration is sufficient for release is contrary to right concentration.

Third working hypothesis: The final step to awakening remains uncertain.

At the end of Chapter 3 we will discuss which working hypotheses have been refuted and which are corroborated.

2.3 References to sources about insight meditation by scholar-monks

In the following paragraphs, we summarize works of some scholar-monks who explain *vipassanā*-meditation with a more analytical approach. Soma Thera, Nyanaponika Thera, Bhikkhu Bodhi, Bhikkhu Sujato and Bhikkhu Anālayo offer many canonical and traditional sources. That distinguishes them from the teachers analysed in the previous sections. The references to canonical sources will be discussed further in Chapter 3, to compare these with the methods taught in the canon or to see whether a specific point is made. We will pay attention to the description of the term *vipassanā*-meditation, its method by following the process as taught, the insight to be gained, the final step to awakening, and the role of calmness or concentration.

2.3.1 Soma Thera

For Soma Thera seeing things according to impermanence etc. is *vipassanā*. 'What sees things in different ways, according to impermanence and the like, is insight; it is a name for wisdom.' (Soma Thera 1961: 358; Patis-a. I, 125). So insight (*vipassanā*) and wisdom are said to be identical.

Soma Thera stresses that the goal of *Nibbāna* can only be reached with the attainment of wisdom by a gradual path, as stated in the *Kīṭāgiri Sutta* (MN 70-I, 479-80) and in AN 8.19 (IV, 201). However, to teach the process Soma Thera points to another *sutta*: 'The order and method of development of the Path is shown in the *Rathavinīta Sutta* of the *Majjhima*-

Nikāya.' (Soma Thera 1961: 353; MN 24-I, 148-50). This *sutta* indicates a process of seven purifications. First one has to be established in the purity of virtue, next the sense doors must be controlled, and then mindfulness to clean the mind and full awareness of all activities should be developed, before one can achieve success in *jhāna*.

Mindfulness belongs to the group of concentration of the Eightfold Path (Soma Thera 1961: 357). Serenity (*samatha*) is a name for concentration; it develops the mind until concentration at least at the level of the first *jhāna* is reached. This level of concentration constitutes the second purification. This concentration is separate from the five hindrances (*nīvaraṇa*) that hinder the development of insight (DN 2-I, 71, 73).[27]

Study and reflection on the Dhamma together with mindfulness and full awareness are necessary to develop wisdom. 'Mindfulness is required in all effective contemplation. Through full awareness one learns to do everything with deliberation' (Soma Thera 1961: 357). One develops wisdom in the next four purifications. 'The last (7th) purification is attained in the Supramundane Path moment when all the factors of the Noble Path occur together.' Having fulfilled wisdom, full sanctity is reached according to Soma Thera.

Serenity and insight (*vipassanā*) have been combined in the *Satipaṭṭhāna-Sutta*s (DN 22 and MN 10). Serenity is produced in these *sutta*s through mindfulness of breathing, although 'both discourses on the foundations of mindfulness lay more stress on the development of insight,' (Soma Thera 1961: 358). Soma Thera equates the method taught in the Noble Eightfold Path to following the order of the seven purifications (Soma Thera 1961: 358-9).

The importance of the first *jhāna* can be based on the Buddha's own awakening, according to MN 36 (I, 246) and on AN 10.1 f (V, 1 f). Of the first *jhāna* it is said that it is the escape from sensuality, due to concentration on what is not connected with sense-desire (Soma Thera 1961: 361). Soma Thera argues as well for the importance of the first *jhāna* on the ground of MN 118: 'The placing of the first tetrad of the *Ānāpānasati-Sutta* at the very beginning of the two main *Satipaṭṭhāna-Sutta*s is a clear indication of the necessity of at least the First *Jhāna,* [to reach] the proper ground for the development of insight' (Soma Thera 1961: 360). He even suggests that all four *jhāna*s are needed, as the Eightfold Path requires right concentration: 'the Buddha has defined Right Concentration,

[27] Soma Thera (1971: 359) also quotes Patis I, 27 to stress that the first *jhāna* suppresses the hindrances. However, that text is not clear without further explanation.

Sammāsamādhi, as the four *jhāna*s, and not anything lower than them.' (Soma Thera 1961: 361) See for example DN 22 (II, 313).

2.3.2 Nyanaponika Thera

According to Nyanaponika (1975 (1962): 44) insight (*vipassanā*) is the highest penetration of truth. 'Insight is the direct and penetrative realization of the Three Characteristics of Existence, i.e. Impermanence, Suffering and Impersonality.' Insight by unshakable personal experience of these characteristics is the purpose and the mind liberating function of the method that he describes. Mindfulness, in its specific aspect of bare attention, provides the key to the distinctive method of *Satipaṭṭhāna* (Nyanaponika 1975 (1962): 30). Within this framework Nyanaponika explains three methods, one is based on the *Mahā-Satipaṭṭhāna-Sutta*, a second offers instructions for mindfulness of breathing, and a third refers to the Burmese way of training.

Right mindfulness equals the four contemplations as taught in *Satipaṭṭhāna.* It includes two modes of practice: bare attention and clear comprehension (*sampajañña*). Nyanaponika (1975 (1962): 36) considers bare attention as fundamental: 'in the light of Bare Attention, the seemingly uniform act of perception will, with increasing clarity, appear as a sequence of numerous and differentiated single phases,'.

Systematic practice centres on a few subjects selected from the contemplations of one's own body. First and foremost is mindfulness of breathing by bare attention to rise and fall and impermanence of the body. Though breathing traditionally is primarily a subject for tranquillity meditation, it can be used also for the development of insight (*vipassanā-bhāvanā*) according to Nyanaponika (1975 (1962): 63).

The second exercise is awareness of one's bodily behaviour when going, standing, sitting or reclining. This is practised both during daily activities and in strict meditative training. Furthermore, one contemplates the impurity of the various parts of the body, to end attachment to the body. Nyanaponika continues with the dissection of the body into the four elements, which underlines the impersonal nature of the body even more. The final exercises on the body concern the cemetery contemplations, either by direct observation of a dead body or by visualization. These are meant to lead to disgust for objects of desire and teach the impermanence of the body.

During all these exercises, bare attention confronts the practitioner with change of events and thus with impermanence. The mind is in a flux and only has a cognizing function, and one cannot detect an individual agent or abiding entity. So one discovers the truth of no-soul or not-self. Any respiratory difficulty makes us aware of suffering.

Mindfulness also shapes the mind by self knowledge and registering harmful thoughts (Nyanaponika 1975 (1962): 39-40). Practising bare attention in daily life will show the possibility of letting go, of abstaining from habitual interfering. Finally, bare attention forges the tool for insight, the experience of impermanence, suffering and impersonality. 'It is the nature of Insight to be free from Desire, Aversion and Delusion, and to see all things as impersonal processes.' (Nyanaponika 1975 (1962): 44)

Right mindfulness includes clear comprehension of purpose and suitability to regulate all action and speech accordant with our ideals and with the highest level of our understanding. Clear comprehension trains in purposeful, circumspect and selfless action (Nyanaponika 1975 (1962): 56). According to Nyanaponika (1975 (1962): 46), it is right knowledge or wisdom (*pañña*) based on right *sati*.

The other three foundations of mindfulness of DN 22 get attention when they come into the range of observation (Nyanaponika 1975 (1962): 58). Feelings are the first reactions to sense impressions, and are just distinguished into pleasant, unpleasant and indifferent sensations. Feelings may give rise to passionate emotions such as craving. However, by bare attention to them one may be able to break the chain of reactions.

The contemplation of the state of the mind gives attention to the condition and the level of consciousness or mind. Beneficial or harmful states of mind are distinguished by bare statements, such as a concentrated mind or a mind with anger.

The contemplation of mental objects, in the sense of contents of thought, will gradually assume the thought forms of the Buddha's teaching. That means, thinking as much as possible in doctrinal terms which are in accordance with what really is and with the goal of liberation (Nyanaponika 1975 (1962): 73). The practice is about observing, within oneself in daily life, the hindrances, fetters or enlightenment factors. One should relate every occurrence to the four Truths.

Morality is the indispensable basis for any higher mental development. Its safest roots lie in the cultivation of the four Sublime States (*brahma-vihāra*), according to Nyanaponika (1975 (1962): 76). It is a primary task of mindfulness to prevent offences against, in particular, loving kindness. By protecting others one protects oneself and vv. (SN 47.19).

Nyanaponika also explains the method for mindfulness of breathing (*Ānāpānasati*). In the first four exercises one observes the distinct beginning, middle and end of the movement of a single breath. His interpretation of the third exercise is 'conscious of the whole breath, I shall breath in-breath out', which means mindfulness throughout all three phases of a breath (Nyanaponika 1975 (1962): 110). With the fourth exercise one calms the breathing.

Furthermore, Nyanaponika offers instructions for the Burmese method of bare insight, which is without first attaining *jhāna*. We summarize his description in section 2.1.9 on Mahāsi Sayādaw. In his chapter on the Burmese *Satipaṭṭhāna* method, Nyanaponika (1975 (1962): 102-4) also describes the relationship between the development of insight and the development of tranquillity (*samatha*). 'The *Development of Tranquillity* aims at the full concentration of mind, attained in the meditative Absorptions (*jhāna*).' (Nyanaponika 1975 (1962): 102)

According to Nyanaponika, discursive thought is absent in higher stages of *jhāna*, and therefore the insight necessary for liberation cannot be reached in that way. Access concentration (*upacāra-samādhi*) is 'attainable in, and necessary for, the successful practice of Insight' (Nyanaponika 1975 (1962): 102-3). Although Nyanaponika acknowledges that the combined method of tranquillity and insight is most frequently described in the scriptures, the method and practice he describes belong, as he admits, to Bare Insight.

As said, Nyanaponika based the above methods on the *Mahā-Satipaṭṭhāna-Sutta* (DN 22) and the *Ānāpānasati-Sutta* (MN 118). Nyanaponika points to his translations of SN 35.70 (IV, 41 ff.) and SN 35.152 (IV, 138 ff.) to support the practice of bare insight.[28] The types of clear comprehension Nyanaponika (1975 (1962): 46) distinguishes are according to the commentaries. Furthermore Nyanaponika (1975 (1962): 139-194) offers many quotes and excerpts from the Pali Canon and some from the commentarial literature, to underline the importance of the four foundations of mindfulness.

[28] Nyanaponika (1975 (1962): 103) refers to his translations nrs. 52 and 53 on pp. 176-8.

2.3.3 Bhikkhu Bodhi

Bhikkhu Bodhi (Nyanaponika and Bhikkhu Bodhi 1999: 25 ff.) describes three stages of training which 'correspond to the threefold division of the Noble Eightfold Path into virtue, concentration and wisdom.' He calls the systematic training to develop wisdom *vipassanā-bhāvanā.* This scholar-monk systematically indicates the relevant *suttas* of the *Aṅguttara-Nikāya.* In this paragraph we refer as well to the numbering of the *suttas* in Nyanaponika Thera and Bhikkhu Bodhi 1999 (N and B), of which Bodhi wrote the introduction explaining his system.

The first stage describes the training in higher virtue for monks, which is based on the code of monastic rules and more informal ways of behaviour, such as restraint of the senses (N and B *sutta* 82=AN 4.165-II, 153). The second stage has been called 'training in the higher mind'. 'The system of meditation prescribed for cultivating concentration is called *samatha-bhāvanā*, the development of tranquillity (14, 72).'[29] These *suttas* with N and B numbers 14 and 72 stress the importance of tranquillity, and many other suttas in the AN mention specific methods related to it.

The meditator must first still the five hindrances for which means are indicated in N and B *suttas* 2, 52 and 111.[30] The most effective means to reach the deepest states of concentration are mindfulness of breathing, and the *kasiṇa* devices which represent the four elements and the primary colours.[31] Bhikkhu Bodhi (1999: 26) seems to indicate that all four *jhānas* must be reached, as he states thus: 'After mastering the fourth jhāna three pathways open up before the meditator.'

The first of the three pathways is to cultivate the formless attainments; the second serves to develop psychic powers and 'superknowledges'. 'And the third is to advance to the next stage of training, the development of wisdom.'(Bodhi in N and B 1999: 26) To provide a foundation for wisdom (*paññā*) is the function of concentration, in the classical structure of the Buddhist path.[32]

---

29 Bodhi in N and B 1999: 25; he refers to *sutta* 14=PTS: AN II, iii, 10 (I, 61) and *sutta* 72=PTS: AN 4.94 (II, 92).

30 *Suttas* 2=AN I, ii, 1-10 (I, 3 ff.); 52 =AN 4.12 (II, 14 f.) and 111=AN 5.193 (III, 230 ff.)

31 N and B *suttas* 196 par. 10=AN 10.60 (V, 111 f.) and 190 par. 4=AN 10.29 (V, 60 f.).

32 However, Bhikkhu Bodhi (in N and B 1999: 27) recognizes that insight may be attained first and tranquillity afterwards, according to *suttas* 72= AN 4.94 (II, 92) and 83=AN 4.170 (II, 156).

The systematic training to develop wisdom is called *vipassanā-bhāvanā*, the development of insight (N and B *suttas* 14 and 72).[33] With a quiet mind a meditator attends mindfully to the body (N and B *sutta* 11=AN I.21.1 ff.-I, 43 ff.). When mindfulness becomes clearer, he or she learns to distinguish the five elements of existence as they arise and pass away (N and B *sutta* 59=AN 4.41-II, 44 ff.). This practice leads to the insight into impermanence. Because the elements of existence are unstable and constantly disintegrating, one realizes these are really concealed forms of suffering (*dukkha*). 'And whatever is impermanent and suffering cannot be identified as a truly existent self.' (Bodhi in N and B 1999: 27)

Impermanence, suffering and not my self are the three universal characteristics of phenomena (N and B *sutta* 48=AN 3.134-I, 286). Because these three are inextricably interwoven, insight into one leads to insight into the others (N and B *suttas* 142 §§ 5-7=AN 7.46-IV, 46 ff.). To contemplate the three characteristics deeply is the essence of insight meditation (Bodhi in N and B 1999: 27; *suttas* 138-40=AN 6.102 ff.-III, 443 f.). The deep knowledge leads the mind to turn away from the five elements of existence with revulsion.

The mind focuses on *Nibbāna*, because that is perceived as the only true security and peace. Revulsion changes into 'dispassion, the fading away of lust and craving, and dispassion in turn culminates in liberation (*vimutti*), the mind's release from all fetters.'[34] The Buddhist path culminates in the destruction of the taints (*āsavas*) of the mind, which means destroying 'sensual craving, craving for existence and ignorance' (N and B *suttas* 131 and 181).[35] When the taints are totally destroyed 'the disciple enters upon "the taintless liberation of the mind, liberation by wisdom, having realized it for himself by direct knowledge" (Bodhi in N and B 1999: 28). This disciple has become an *Arahant*, a worthy one.

2.3.4 Bhikkhu Sujato

Bhikkhu Sujato offers the following definition: '*Vipassanā* is the seeing and exploring of activities. It therefore refers to wisdom in its refined mode of investigation into the nature of reality as experience.'[36] Sujato

[33] N and B *suttas* 14=AN 2.3.10 (I, 61) and 72=AN 4.94 (II, 92).

[34] Bodhi in N and B 1999: 27; N and B *suttas* 128=AN 6.52 (III, 362 ff.); 182=AN 10.1 (V, 1 f.) and 183=AN 10. 2-V, 2 ff.

[35] N and B *suttas* 131=AN 6.63 (III, 410 ff.) and 181=AN 9.36 (IV, 421 ff.).

[36] Sujato 2010: Ch. 2, pages not numbered; Sujato 2001: 26.

notes three important aspects of *vipassanā*. Firstly, the penetrative, clear-eyed observation of what is occurring in the present moment. And secondly, he mentions the ability to infer a correct conclusion by closely examining the evidence before one's eyes, understanding it in line with valid general principles. Thirdly, *vipassanā* brings about the fading of ignorance, a term for the intellectual aspect of the defilements.

Sujato describes the process to develop insight according to MN 10 as follows: 'Each exercise included in the four establishings of mindfulness concludes with a passage describing three aspects of insight development.' (Sujato 2001: 48) He calls this the 'insight refrain' which explains how these practices should be applied. Sujato takes this refrain as a framework to describe the process of how to practice, although he admits doubts about it as the refrain varies considerably between the different renderings of *satipaṭṭhāna*.

a) The refrain begins with contemplating the body in the body within himself and externally. This is explained in *sutta* MN 118 as the in-and-out breaths are a certain body (Sujato 2001: 35).

b) The second aspect of insight development in the refrain of MN 10 is the contemplation of the principles of origination and dissolution. Sujato (2001: 51) quotes another *sutta*, SN 47.42,[37] which offers a description of these principles:

> "The body originates due to the origination of nutriment; the body ends due to the cessation of nutriment. Feelings originate due to the origination of contact; feelings end due to the cessation of contact. The mind originates due to the origination of mentality and physical form; the mind ends due to the cessation of mentality and physical form. Dhammas originate due to the origination of attention; dhammas end due to the cessation of attention."

The origin of feelings is said to be 'contact', perhaps 'stimulus' would be a better rendering of the Pali *phassa*. In saying that *dhamma*s are originated by attention, the Buddha is pointing out, in particular according to Sujato, the relation between the five hindrances and the seven enlightenment factors. The enlightenment factors and the other categories included in the contemplation of *dhamma*s are developed by 'paying attention to the

[37] PTS: SN XLVII, III, V, ii (V, 184).

root' or to the essence. 'By bringing in the investigation into causality so explicitly here, the Buddha is emphasizing the strong role that wisdom plays in this final of the four satipaṭṭhānas.'[38]

c) Mindfulness should not lead to a deeper contemplation than necessary to establish direct knowledge. 'The third aspect of insight development involves the establishing of mindfulness only for a measure of knowledge and mindfulness.'[39] Which kind of knowledge is meant here? 'The interpretation of the vipassanā schools would bring in the so-called 'insight-knowledges' here. But this list dates from many centuries after the Buddha and cannot have been meant here.' (Sujato 2010 Ch. 3) *Sutta* AN 6.64 (IV, 417 ff.) details the kinds of knowledge obtainable by *satipaṭṭhāna*, especially the various kinds of psychic knowledge, such as how beings pass on according to their actions.

d) Sujato (2001: 48) mentioned three aspects of insight development, and describes two more (Sujato 2001: 57). The final step of these knowledges is, according to Sujato's translation and numbering:

> "I enter and abide, due to the evaporation of the poisons, in the poison-free release of heart, release by understanding, having witnessed it here and now with my own direct knowledge."
>
> (SN 52.24)[40]

e) The refrains of the *Satipaṭṭhāna Sutta* conclude with the following statement, which Sujato counts as part of the insight section: "One abides independent, not grasping at anything in the world." (MN 10-I, 57 ff.; DN 22-II, 291 ff.) This may refer to either the comprehensive detachment from any aspect of existence (see MN 143), or to stream-entry. The latter possibility is expressed in the following *sutta* passage: "The four *satipaṭṭhāna*s are taught and described by me for the abandoning and surmounting of these dependencies on views connected with former times and dependencies on views connected with times to come." (DN 29-III, 141) These views which should be overcome by *satipaṭṭhāna*, concern our 'self' as an identical, unchanging essence existing in past and in future

[38] 'Attention' is featured in the context of dependent origination, for example DN 14 (II, 30 f).

[39] Sujato 2001: 57; for further interpretation see Anālayo 2003: 112-3.

[40] PTS: SN LII, VIII, II, xiv (V, 305 f.)

lives. Thus Sujato (2001: 58) links the foundations of mindfulness with the 'this is not-the-self' doctrine.

Sujato stresses the point that *samatha* must be developed as well as *vipassanā*; for him these two qualities constitute a comprehensive summary of the meditative aspect of the path. *Vipassanā* and *samatha* almost always occur as a pair in the *suttas*, they are a pair of mental qualities to be developed by means of the eightfold path. Sujato (2001: 27) argues this point by quoting *sutta* AN 2.3.10-I, 61, which stresses the equal importance of calm and insight:

> "Monks, these two principles share in realization. What two? Samatha and vipassanā. When samatha is developed, what purpose is achieved? The mind is developed. When the mind is developed, what purpose is achieved? Lust is abandoned. When vipassanā is developed, what purpose is achieved? Understanding is developed. When understanding is developed, what purpose is achieved? Ignorance is abandoned."

According to Sujato the meditation methods taught in the *suttas* are not distinguished as either concentration or *vipassanā* practices. *Samatha* and *vipassanā* were considered as mental conditions rather than methods. 'In the *suttas*, no meditation technique is labeled, such as by saying

> "*kasiṇas* and loving-kindness are *samatha, satipaṭṭhāna* is *vipassanā*"'. A growing tendency to segregate and systematize the various meditation subjects developed into the prevailing practice of identifying *samatha* and *vipassanā* with the meditation subjects themselves, rather than with the mental qualities which the techniques foster.'

In AN 4.170 (II, 156 f.), Venerable Ānanda also states that enlightenment must depend on some combination of *samatha* and *vipassana*. But the order of development of these two may be different, as exemplified in the following *suttas*: MN 149 (III, 289–90); AN 4.94 (II, 93 ff.); AN 9.4 (IV, 357), and AN 10.54 (V, 98 ff.).

Sujato (2001: 87) asserts that practice should be gradual: 'Of all the versions of the gradual training none can rival the *Sāmaññaphala-Sutta*' (DN 2). He offers long quotes from this *sutta*. However, he has based the description of *vipassanā* practice on MN 10.

The essence of practice according to Sujato (2010, end of Ch. 5) is developing the balance and harmony between *jhāna* and wisdom, the emotional and intellectual qualities. Sujato quotes a verse from the *Dhammapāda*:

> "There's no jhāna for one without wisdom,
> No wisdom for one without jhāna;
> But for one with both jhāna and wisdom,
> Nibbana surely is near." (Dhp 372)

According to Sujato (2010, Ch. 3), 'DN 22 is nothing more than a late expansion of MN 10;' and the four noble Truths were taken from MN 141. Sujato indicates *Sutta*s DN 22, MN 141, and SN 45.8 (XLV, I, I, viii-V, 10) as sources for 'right *samādhi*', which describe this stage of the Path as the four *jhāna*s. Furthermore, Sujato underlines the importance of the fourth *jhāna* with a quote from AN 10.20 (V, 29 ff.), in which the following is said of a monk:

> "...he enters and abides in the fourth *jhāna*; has mind well released with the abandoning of lust, anger, and delusion; and has understanding well released by understanding that lust, anger, and delusion have been permanently uprooted. Whatever noble ones that lived in the past, will live in the future, or are living now, all of them live according to these ten ways of noble living."

However, Sujato also refers to several *sutta*s in which the first *jhāna* is shown to be the minimum necessary to become an *Arahant* (MN 64; AN 9.36-IV, 421 ff.).

In an e-book we accessed in 2013, Sujato mentions the *Chachakka-Sutta* (MN 148) which is relevant to our subject, although not part of his method to reach *vipassanā*. According to Sujato (2012: 318), 'The Theravāda version is one of the most incisive texts dealing purely with insight in the canon. The elegance of form and profundity of content argue for its authenticity.' This discourse expounds six groups of six *dhamma*s to explain how craving arises, impermanence and not my self. Abandoning feelings one can arouse true knowledge.

2.3.5 Bhikkhu Anālayo

According to Bhikkhu Anālayo (2010: 83), 'the early Buddhist conception of *vipassanā* (which) stands for "liberating insight", that is, for the type of insight whose growth culminates in the total release of the mind from the grip of defilements and delusion.' Real insight needs to be based on a sound moral foundation and development of tranquility (*samatha*).

Mindfulness of breathing can be employed to develop insight and tranquillity.[41] One can develop tranquillity by just mentally knowing the presence of the breath. Deeper stages of tranquillity eclipse the attraction of sensual desires (MN 14-I, 91; MN 43-I, 294; MN 75-I, 504 ff.; AN 2.3.10-I, 61; AN 2.17.3 ff.-I, 100; AN 5.176-III, 207 and AN 9.33 IV, 411). The *Itivuttaka* as well states that tranquillity is needed to prevent sense desires thus:

> 'Those who by mindfully meditating with calm and discerning mind properly see the teaching with insight and are no longer interested in sensuality.'(It 39-40, *sutta* 45)

On this base the development of insight towards liberating insight (*vipassanā*) can begin. According to Anālayo (2010: 88): 'Once sensuality has been left behind, the growth of dispassion as a net result of deepening insight will also affect one's attitude to the meditative experience itself.' Besides he argues the need for calm as a base to develop insight thus: 'The development of tranquillity leads to a high degree of mastery over the mind and thereby forms the basis for the development of insight.' (Anālayo 2010: 108). However, both the level of tranquillity needed before beginning the development of insight and the order of developing these two qualities are undetermined (AN 4.170-II,157).

One of the methods to develop insight consists in observing different aspects of the process of breathing. First penetrative awareness (*vipassaṁ*) of the impermanent nature of reality must be developed (Th 1091). 'Comprehensive insight into impermanence then needs to lead on to insight into unsatisfactoriness and not-self or emptiness (Th 1117).' (Anālayo 2010: 84) That which is impermanent because of that quality is unsatisfactory. So according to MN 22 (I, 138), it is not appropriate to see 'what is impermanent, unsatisfactory and subject to change as "this is mine, this I am,

[41] According to MN 43 (I, 294), MN 149 (III, 289) and AN 4.146 f. (II, 140) etc. tranquillity and insight both have to be developed.

this is myself".' This is a method of meditation according to Anālayo (2010: 85): 'Needless to say, passages like this are guided forms of meditation for the development of liberating insight.'

A presentation in AN 5.72 (III, 85 f.) combines the scope of insight into impermanence, unsatisfactoriness and not-self, with the perception of eradication of the defilements in the mind and perception of dispassion. Eradication of the defilements seems equivalent to the destruction of the fluxes (*āsava*s). In him who knows and sees the *āsava*s are extinct (SN 12.23-II, 30). The same *sutta* might be quoted to support the following remark. The accomplishment of dispassion is the proximate cause for liberation (Anālayo 2010: 85).

Furthermore, Anālayo '(2010: 86) points to the investigation-of-phenomena awakening factor as a 'quality of particular relevance for the development of insight.' He refers to MN 118 (III, 85). *Sutta* AN 6.17 (III, 301) summarizes the conditions for awakening. The *Itivuttaka* (It I-3) indicates that the defilements have to be understood and abandoned with insight.

Other qualities associated with *vipassanā* are attention to a matter at hand and the ability to remain in the present moment (MN 133-III, 193). The practices of the *Satipaṭṭhāna Sutta* (MN 10-I, 56) to establish mindfulness 'point to the important support that the development of mindfulness can offer to the growth of insight.' (Anālayo 2010: 91-98). Besides, this *sutta* uses the verb form *pajānāti,* he or she knows, in relation to mindfulness. The same word is in AN 4.65 (II, 71) and Th 472 referring to one who sees with insight. Although Anālayo does not intend to limit insight to mindfulness practice, he describes certain practices of the *Satipaṭṭhāna Sutta* which are useful to develop insight.

Sutta SN 47.40 [42] states that contemplating arising and passing away is a necessary condition for the development (*bhāvanā*) of *satipaṭṭhāna.* This is highlighted in the refrain after each exercise of MN 10. Mindfulness of breathing demonstrates the impermanence of existence and the dependence of life on the next breath. What 'formerly was 'my body' can with growing insight be seen as a conglomeration of the four elements.' Contemplation of the changing nature of feelings is another method to gain the insights of impermanence and of not my self (MN 140-III, 244; DN 15-II, 67).

[42] PTS: SN XLVII, III, IV, x (V, 183).

When one is able to see an absorption as rising and falling or a conditioned product of the mind, one will reach such insight that either non-return or awakening can be expected (MN 111-III, 25; MN 52-I, 350). Insight into impermanence of the five constituents of a 'person' features in many discourses as a last step to liberation (DN 14-II, 35; DN 33-III, 223; SN 18.22-II, 253; AN 4.41-II, 45 and AN 8.2-IV, 153). This erodes the foundation of clinging to a self.

The last exercises in the *Satipaṭṭhāna Sutta* concern insight in the four noble Truths. This forms 'the culmination of the growth of insight' as, according to Anālayo (2010: 98), it equals full insight into the dependent arising of *dukkha* and its cessation. According to MN 56 (I, 380) it leads to the *Dhamma*-vision "whatever is of the nature to uprise, all that is of the nature to stop", which implies stream entry, and in MN 4 (I, 23) insight in the four noble Truths leads to full awakening. True insight into the four noble Truths further requires that craving be abandoned, that the cessation of craving has to be realized and that the eightfold path has been developed (SN LVI, XII, III, v-V, 422; SN LVI, XII, III, vii-V, 436).

The definition of right concentration as a factor of the noble eightfold Path, which is most frequently found, describes the four absorptions. However, according to several discourses the first absorption suffices to attain awakening. Anālayo (2010: 132) mentions MN 52 (I, 350), MN 64 (I, 435); AN 9.36 (IV, 422) and AN 11.17 (V, 343). Anyway, the early discourses seem not to offer support for the 'dry insight' approach as a possibility to reach awakening without *jhāna* (Anālayo 2010: 135).[43]

Still, several discourses mention the importance of hearing or knowledge of, and reflection on, the *Dhamma* for the development of insight (MN 56-I, 380; AN II, 157, AN 8.2-IV, 151; Ud 49; Vin II, 192). Anālayo (2010: 91) remarks that in the early discourses *vipassanā* stands predominantly for insight as a quality to be developed and not for a specific meditation technique.

2.4 Summary of the methods of the scholar-monks

Soma Thera and Bhikkhu Sujato both teach gradual processes, referring to many canonical texts. Both agree as well that the first *jhāna* is the min-

[43] 'Dry insight' refers to a method to reach insight without reaching a state of meditative absorption (*jhāna*).

imum necessary to reach insight and enlightenment, according to the *suttas*. Sujato stresses the point that *samatha* must be developed in balance with *vipassanā*. Soma Thera follows the order of the seven purifications in his approach, while Sujato uses the refrain of the *Satipaṭṭhāna Sutta* as a framework to develop insight. Sujato also refers to the *Chachakka-Sutta* (MN 148) as a discourse dealing with insight.

For Nyanaponika Thera *vipassanā* means insight by unshakable personal experience of the three characteristics of existence, this is the purpose and the mind liberating function of the method. Mindfulness is the main aspect of the practice of bare attention to rise and fall and impermanence of the body, whether explained by means of the *Mahā-Satipaṭṭhāna-Sutta* or through the Burmese way of training. Nyanaponika also explains the method for mindfulness of breathing (*Ānāpānasati*) thus: one distinguishes in the movement of a single breath the beginning, middle and end. According to Nyanaponika, access concentration (*upacāra-samādhi*) is 'attainable in, and necessary for, the successful practice of Insight'.

Bhikkhu Bodhi systematically describes three stages of training in virtue, concentration and wisdom based on *sutta*s of the *Aṅguttara-Nikāya*. Concentration is a necessity; Bodhi seems to indicate that the fourth *jhāna* should be reached. Mindful attention to the body and then to the five elements of existence develop insight into the three characteristics of existence, according to Bodhi.

Bhikkhu Anālayo stresses that real insight needs to be based on a sound moral foundation and that such insight requires the development of tranquility. He describes two sequences leading to insight based on discourses. However, Anālayo like Sujato noted that *vipassanā* was often seen in the discourses as a mental quality. Insight in impermanence is the starting point in the development of wisdom for Anālayo, it can lead to insight in unsatisfactoriness and not-self. An alternative way follows the *Satipaṭṭhāna* exercises, for example observing the process of breathing. However, development of insight should not be limited to mindfulness practice. According to Anālayo, the early discourses seem not to offer support for the 'dry insight' approach as a possibility to reach awakening without *jhāna*. The first *jhāna* may be sufficient to attain awakening.

To avoid too much repetition, we will discuss the references of the scholar-monks to *sutta*s in the next chapter.

Chapter 3

Recent teachings about *Vipassanā*-meditation compared with Pali *sutta*s

This chapter considers the relationships between the methods as described in Chapter 2 and those Pali canonical sources, in particular *sutta*s, which are either mentioned by the teachers and scholar-monks or those which seem at first sight implied.

First we analyse a teaching or explanation, concentrating on the process.

Secondly, we suggest some conclusions and remarks on the relationships between that method and the canonical sources, in an indented section with a horizontal line in front: —

Thirdly, we do the same with the explanations of the scholar-monks.

Fourthly, we offer conclusions on the comparison of recent *Vipassanā* teachings with Pali *sutta*s and on the working hypotheses of Chapter 2. Differences with canonical sources do not imply the method of any of the teachers discussed is wrong, as it may be a very useful development to get (lay) people started on the meditation path. In other cases the descriptions used here may be incomplete.

3.1 Analysis of the teachings and related *sutta*s

We begin with a brief analysis of the method a teacher proposed. Secondly, we comment on the conformity or difference with the indicated or obviously relevant *sutta*s.

3.1.1 Give up attachment according to Ajahn Chah

Ajahn Chah rarely explicitly referred to a *sutta* in our sources. However, he taught that the practice of mindfulness of breathing (*Ānāpānasati*) is a course for the development of morality, concentration and wisdom (Ajahn Chah 1982: 15, 20). So we suggest that primarily the method of MN 118 is relevant, but DN 22 and MN 10 explain attention to the breath as well.

Through the practice of *Vipassanā*- or insight meditation we must develop attention to the mind, Ajahn Chah taught. If there is mindfulness there will be clear comprehension, and in general wisdom will arise. Then we see that happy or sad states of mind are impermanent (*anicca*) as the basis, but unsatisfactory (*dukkha*) as well, and that there is no individual entity (*anattā*).

Sīla and a moderate level of concentration have supporting parts, which are not necessarily developed before insight practice starts. Still, according to an interview with Ajahn Chah, *sīla* or discipline and morality are essential to support our practice; the intention is the main aspect. Ajahn Chah develops calmness (*samatha*) by mindfulness of the in-and-out-breath. Calmness meditation leads to a peaceful and happy mind. However, this as well should be seen with wisdom as not lasting. So we should not cling to calmness because that causes suffering. Practice leads to giving up all attachment. Finally we understand the four Truths. The three groups of the Path *sīla, samādhi* and *paññā* work together forming one whole, which provides the energy that gives rise to *vipassanā* (insight knowledge). *Sati* has to be continuously maintained, whatever you do (Ajahn Chah 1991: 20-1).

— *Sutta*s MN 118, DN 22, and MN 10 seem most relevant to the practice Ajahn Chah teaches. MN 10 and MN 118 only mention the contemplation of rising and falling or impermanence, but do not connect it to *dukkha* and *anattā*. The *sutta*s DN 22, MN 10, and MN 118 do not teach that only mindfulness of the in-and-out-breath is sufficient, but other exercises in these *sutta*s are attention to the body, to feelings, to the mind and to mental factors. Understanding the four Truths has not been elaborated in MN 118 or MN 10. Among the *sutta*s just mentioned, only in DN 22 a method leading to understanding of the four Truths has been explained. In that *sutta* the mental factors include the four Truths, culminating in the development of the four *jhāna*s. These types of concentration are also elaborated in DN 22. However, Ajahn Chah did not think that absorption, implying the *jhāna*s, is necessary. So the method of Ajahn Chah is not fully in line with either DN 22 or MN 10 or MN 118.

3.1.2 Insight into the essence of existence according to Bhikkhu Mettavīhari

According to Mettavīhari, *Vipassanā* means insight into the real essence of existence. One should observe the four foundations of mindfulness during exercises for '*vipassanā*-meditation': sitting, going, standing, bowing and laying down. The core of the practice consists in constant awareness. 'The full time observation of yourself is true *vipassanā*- practice.'

One has to develop insight by following the order of the sixteen *ñāṇa*s. Mettavīhari connects this system of knowledge with the seven stages of purification, in which the sixth is the purity of insight-knowledge of the Path (*patipadā-ñāṇadassana-visudhi*) consisting of the progress from the 4th to the 12th *vipassanā ñāṇa*s. Mettavīhari refers to merit in former lives as a requirement for the stages of *ñāṇa* beyond the 12th. The system culminates in the 14th *ñāṇa* when one sees easily the passing away of *nāma-rūpa* without worldly consciousness. There is no explicit mention of calmness meditation.

— To observe the four foundations of mindfulness, without specific explanation of concentration or calmness meditation, fits the *Satipaṭṭhāna-Sutta* (MN 10). Thereby we suppose that 'to observe' means to be aware or to contemplate.

Mettavīhari taught to follow the order of the sixteen *ñāṇa*s (types of knowledge). However, according to Anālayo (2001: 99) a systematic survey of the insight knowledges is not found in the early discourses. We agree, as we could not trace the list of the sixteen *ñāṇa*s or ten insight knowledges in a *sutta*. A.K. Warder (1982: xxi), the author of the introduction to the English translation of the *Paṭisambhidāmagga*, suggests these were first treated in that work, and they were later known in the Theravāda tradition as the 'insight knowledges'. Although this work is part of the *Sutta-Piṭāka*, the chapters dealing with these knowledges are not indicated as *sutta*s.

As contemplating origination and dissolution is part of the practice taught in MN 10 as well, this *sutta* agrees with the aspect impermanence in Mettavīhari's method. We conclude that an important part of the practice Mettavīhari taught agrees with MN 10, and the development of the sixteen *ñāṇa*s follows a later Theravāda tradition.

3.1.3 Dynamic meditation by Luangpor Teaan

Luangpor Teaan uses the movement of the body to develop awareness (*sati*), first of the body, of feelings, and then of thoughts. *Vipassanā*-meditation is explicitly mentioned in the chapter on Luangpor Teaan by Bannaruji (2006: 67-75). Luangpor Teaan stresses the relationship with the four foundations of mindfulness, to be developed in the usual order of the (*Mahā-*)*Satipaṭṭhāna-Sutta*. In the second foundation total awareness of body and mind arises, leading to equanimity of feelings. The fourth foundation implies total awareness of body and mind and '*samathi*' (steadiness of mind) arises, this leads to liberating knowledge (*paññā*) and one sees the cause of suffering. The highest state is 'arising-extinguishing of the mind'.

— According to the *Mahā-Satipaṭṭhāna-Sutta*, in whatever way the body is disposed, one has full awareness and comprehension that it is acting in that way (DN 22 (II, 292). But how are the other practices of DN 22 developed in the method of Luangpor Teaan? The description of Bannaruji (2006) does not make that explicit.

Besides, it is problematic in the system taught by Luangpor that total awareness of body and mind are already believed to exist in the 2nd foundation of mindfulness. Furthermore, total awareness of body and mind seems difficult to reconcile with arising-extinguishing of the mind, which is called the final step to awakening in his practice. The development of *samathi* may point to DN 22 (II, 291), but not necessarily to right concentration such as in DN 22 (II, 313).

3.1.4 Look inside as taught by Venerable Hiran

Ven. Hiran is a 'forest monk' trying to limit theory to what is necessary for progress in meditation. *Vipassanā*-meditation is contemplating the inside of the body. Concentrate on the dominant feeling in the body. If you study pain, you will note that nothing lasts long. This will lead one to see impermanence and the other two characteristics *dukkha* and *anattā*. This is *vipassanā* insight.

— Since the method explained above is based on oral communication by Ven. Hiran, it is meant to be a practical step and does not claim to be a complete theoretical system. So comparison with the *Mahāsatipaṭṭhāna-Sutta*, which Ven. Hiran mentioned as a framework, is not useful.

3.1.5 Observe sitting *rūpa* in Boonkanjanaram meditation centre

Notwithstanding the theoretical complexity of the system, the *vipassanā*-meditation practice in Boonkanjanaram is not complicated. The basic idea is that our own bodies are the most obvious source of suffering. Be aware of all positions of the body (called *rūpa*); mainly observe sitting *rūpa* and change with right understanding to walking *rūpa* to cure sitting *rūpa*'s suffering. The system of the sixteen *ñaṇās* offers the explanation of progress. *Vipassanā ñāṇa* consists in numbers 4 to 12 of the system of sixteen *ñāṇas*. The highest *vipassanā* insight occurs in the 12th *ñaṇā*, in which *dukkha-sacca* and *samudaya-sacca* are realized. Right Understanding (*sammā-diṭṭhi*) of the four Noble Truths, as attained in the 14th *ñaṇā*, makes it possible to reach the highest stage, *Arahatta-magga*. Only momentary concentration is deemed to be necessary for *vipassanā*-practice.

The book *Vipassanā Bhavana* (1988: 104) used at Boonkanjanaram refers to the *Kāyānupassanā Satipaṭṭhāna*. Other references are to the *Mahāsatipaṭṭhāna-Sutta* (DN 22) and the *Visuddhimagga*.

— The practice taught at Boonkanjanaram is simple. Because of the central concern for the positions of the body in the practice, it seems useful to look to the *Kāyagatāsati-Sutta*. In particular the attention to positions of the body in MN 119 (III, 90-3) is relevant for this system.[44] That practice teaches to note suffering and impermanence. However, part of the system of MN 119 consists of development of the four *jhānas* as well, while in Boonkanjanaram momentary concentration is deemed sufficient to develop insight.

Mindfulness directed to the body, if practiced and made much of, is deemed to give great benefit according to AN 1.21.1 ff. (I, 43-46). Those benefits include mindfulness, ignorance is abandoned, and this method conduces to comprehensive insight. "They

[44] In Boonkanjaranam the body is called *rūpa*. "*Kāya*" in *suttas* such as MN 118 and MN 119 may have a somewhat wider meaning, as the main, respectively the first practice concerns breathing. This aspect received no special attention in the method of Boonkanjaranam.

have realized the Deathless who have realized mindfulness directed to the body." (Nyanaponika and Bodhi 1999: 38-40)

The theoretical explanation by means of the sixteen *ñaṇā*s is similar to Mettavīhari's method. So it may be based on the *Paṭisambhidāmagga*, and it is also found in the later Theravāda tradition of the *Visuddhimagga*.

The *Mahāsatipaṭṭhāna-Sutta* (DN 22) teaches many exercises and the four *jhāna*s as part of its method, not only momentary concentration. So the *sutta*s to which this method refers, require more concentration than the practice taught at Boonkanjanaram.

3.1.6 Continuous awareness according to Dhiravamsa

Dhiravamsa teaches that insight meditation by means of the way of the *Satipaṭṭhāna-Sutta* (MN 10) leads to destruction of suffering and attainment of *Nibbāna*. The starting object for *Vipassanā* or insight meditation is the movement up and down of the belly with the breath. The instruction for the practice is 'to be constantly aware and mindful of whatever is arising in or entering the consciousness and body, knowing them for what they are without conceptualizing, labelling, or analyzing things into categories.'

Vipassanā-meditation consists of five factors: exertion of energy into the present moment; clear seeing what is happening at the present moment; choiceless and desireless awareness; letting go of what is pleasurable, and of self image; maintaining an attitude of non-attachment to experiences and possessions.

The process of arising and passing away makes impermanence and interdependence clear. Direct perception and insight into the three characteristics of existence (according to Dhiravamsa: impermanence, dissatisfactory nature, and voidness) destroy the idea of an eternal self. Impeccable, full awareness in every moment of living may be 'enlightenment'. However, to become an *Arahant* requires a higher level of insight leading to the destruction of any clinging. Concentration meditation does not lead to insight.

— Dhiravamsa's method follows parts of the *Satipaṭṭhāna-Sutta* (MN 10). A difference with MN 10 is that contemplation does not play a role, and in particular the contemplation of the mental factors is not developed. However, just knowing what arises and passes away in the body and consciousness fits the refrain of that *sutta* well. So, the connection with impermanence is logical.

How to develop insight in the 'dissatisfactory nature' is less evident. *Dukkha* is indeed one of the contemplations of mental factors in MN 10. However, Dhiravamsa does not teach these mental factors.

In his method, concentration has no part in developing direct insight into impermanence, dissatisfactory nature, and voidness. Dhiravamsa mentions 'voidness' as one of the characteristics of existence. The concept of 'voidness' is mentioned in the *Paṭisambhidāmagga* as a characteristic of existence, besides it becomes a central concept in certain Mahāyāna-*sūtra*s, but it does not figure in MN 10.

3.1.7 Seven stages of purification as taught by Flickstein

Flickstein interprets insight meditation as experience of the characteristics of existence. The goal of insight meditation is to see the things as they really are. Right view and right thought are related to the development of insight. Flickstein combines the seven stages of purification of MN 24 with their elaboration in the *Visuddhimagga,* and with the exercises of DN 22 in his method. He admits this has no foundation in the canon. He follows systematically all practices of DN 22, and he explains many exercises related to these practices. Furthermore one experiences the 16 stages of intuitive insight. Access concentration calms the mind and suppresses the hindrances temporarily, so we can start insight meditation. However, momentary concentration is sufficient as well. 'Contemplation' refers to mindfulness and insight meditation instead of cognitive reflection according to this method.

— The strong points of Flickstein's method are that he follows all practices of DN 22 and offers many exercises, which he explains in detail. However, these exercises may not all be canonical. To start with 'right view' as intellectual understanding of the four Noble Truths and finally reaching intuitive and direct awareness of their meaning is a useful explanation. Combining the seven stages of purification of MN 24 with their elaboration in the *Visuddhimagga,* and with the exercises of DN 22 has no foundation in the canon. It may also complicate Flickstein's method too much, especially as one is supposed to experience the sixteen stages of intuitive insight as well. These complexities seem to lead to some contradictions. For example, purification by knowledge and insight regarding the Path is said to be the last stage before *Nibbāna*, but 'purification by knowledge and insight' comes next and leads to the supra-mundane. Notwithstanding Flickstein's arguments for the need of access concentration before insight training, momentary concentration is deemed sufficient as well.

Another problem concerns the interpretation of contemplation. When a monk contemplates the five elements of existence according to DN 22 (II, 301) the text reads: 'Here, a monk thinks: "such is form, such is the arising of form,"' etc. (Walshe 1987: 342). This means cognitive reflection. However, Flickstein interprets contemplation as mindfulness and insight meditation, which he explains as experience of the characteristics of existence. So, Flickstein's interpretation of contemplation apparently disagrees with DN 22.

3.1.8 Christina Feldman teaches mindfulness of changing experiences

According to Feldman *vipassanā* practice should include the four foundations of mindfulness of the *Satipaṭṭhāna-Sutta* (MN 10). She teaches to be in touch with changing experiences to gain insight into the impermanence, the selfless nature, and the suffering character of these experiences. Insight can develop as well on the basis of the *Ānāpānasati-Sutta* (MN 118). Momentary concentration on any object that arises is a sufficient level of concentration.

— This practice implies similar differences with MN 10 as we mentioned in the discussion of Dhiravamsa's teaching: contemplation of the mental factors is not developed, as we only should be in touch with changing experiences. Does insight in the suffering and selfless nature of the experiences arise automatically? However, impermanence agrees well with the refrain of *sutta* MN 10.

3.1.9 Mahāsi Sayādaw stresses bare noticing of the rising and falling of the abdomen

Vipassanā-meditation involves, according to Mahāsi Sayādaw, first and foremost quietly noting the rising and falling of the abdomen during breathing. In this exercise 'noting' refers to observing and mentally naming "rising and falling". Next, noting each thought and action is taught. There should be general mindfulness of the four postures during the day, and noticing all activities and feelings. According to Nyanaponika, it is allowed to change posture if the pain persists, then the practice of mindful walking is recommended. One develops the steadfast insight, without reflection, that all the psycho-physical factors are *anicca*, *dukkha* and *anattā*. This will lead to a noble one to arise. Then, as faith, energy, mindfulness, concentration, and wisdom are balanced, one will realize *Nibbāna*.

Awareness develops the necessary concentration. However, Mahāsi only mentioned this in passing, which may have led to different interpretations of his method, as mentioned in 2.1.9. The right way for mind-training by contemplation is found in the *Mahāsatipaṭṭhāna-Sutta*. The stages of insight 'rising-extinction of *nāma* and *rūpa*', and 'impermanence of *nāma* and *rūpa*' have been specified. Seeing that this happens independent of our will, may lead to the knowledge of the non-self of *nāma* and *rūpa*.

— Mahāsi mentioned DN 22; however he follows some but not all its exercises. Insight in impermanence fits that training. However, contemplation of the mental factors requires more than bare noting. Among these mental factors DN 22 teaches the development of the four states of right concentration, on which Mahāsi offers no explicit training. The attention to breathing is the core subject of the *Ānāpānasati-Sutta* (MN 118). So MN 118 seems nearer to his practice, but concerning *dukkha* and *anattā* this *sutta* is silent.

3.1.10 Buddhadasa Bhikkhu taught to follow the breath at the nose

The *vipassanā*-meditation techniques of Buddhadasa are apparently centred on attention to breathing. One should follow the breath at the nose. Contemplation of breathing makes clear that we do not control the five elements of existence, so these are impermanent and non-self. Seeing the impermanence of the five elements of existence appears to be the core insight which is the result and that eventually leads to getting rid of the defilements.

Still, becoming a 'noble one' does not mean that the meditator is already an *Arahant*. The final step to *Nibbāna* has not been specified, but we may learn about it from nature around us. Concentration below the level of the first *jhāna* may be developed by following the breath, before starting with *vipassanā* practice.

— The *vipassanā*-meditation technique of Buddhadasa is related to the *Ānāpānasati-Sutta* (MN 118), which text explains attention to the breath. The steps generally follow those in the *sutta*. Where the breath is to be examined is left open in that *sutta*, in the method considered the breath is examined at the tip of the nose. *Sutta* MN 118 indeed stresses impermanence.

However, next MN 118 (III, 85-8) teaches how to develop the seven factors of awakening, the final one of which is equanimity. These can lead to real knowledge and liberation. Attention to the five elements of existence seems not mentioned in that *sutta* to get rid of the defilements. So the later stages of Buddhadasa's training are not the same as those taught in MN 118. Still, methods to develop insight related to the five elements of existence have been taught in canonical texts such as the *Vinaya*, (the 'second teaching' argues that we do not control the five elements of existence) and MN 22.

3.1.11 Bhikkhu Gunaratana balances attentiveness and concentration

The core of *vipassanā*-meditation is to be attentive according to Gunaratana. Attention to the breath following the *Ānāpānasati-Sutta* (MN 118) is his preferred method of *vipassanā*-meditation. He also teaches attention to the breath for concentration. Even when only mindfulness of the body is established following MN 118, one can practice the seven factors of enlightenment. Concentration needs to be developed in balance with mindfulness. Only while in concentration at the level of *jhāna* you can see reality. During insight meditation one can experience the three characteristics of existence and final peace, *nibbāna*.

— Gunaratana makes an effort to avoid listing many points. The *Ānāpānasati-Sutta* (MN 118-III, 86) states that when the four forms of cultivation of mindfulness are developed in such a way, and if a monk contemplates the body in the manner prescribed, attention is developed and established. So this section may be interpreted as Gunaratana suggests.

However, MN 118 does not teach explicitly to see *dukkha* and *anattā*. Furthermore, Gunaratana states that the joy and happiness developed in MN 118 are not *jhāna*, but he does not explain how to reach that necessary level of concentration. The description of the first *jhāna* seems useful to indicate the way and the difference with MN 118:

> "Here, a monk, detached from sense desires, detached from unwholesome mental states, enters and remains in the first jhāna, which is with thinking and pondering, born of detachment, filled with delight and joy."
>
> (DN 22-II, 313, transl. Walshe 1987)

So, not all factors relevant for *jhāna* are mentioned in MN 118.

3.1.12 Pa Auk teaches to see ultimate materiality

Pa Auk Sayādaw interprets *vipassanā*-meditation as seeing clearly ultimate materiality. He teaches mindfulness of breathing, *ānāpānasati*, to train systematically the awareness of the breath. This seems to be his preferred approach. Pa Auk trains *samatha* according to the *Ānāpānasati-Sutta* (MN 118). When the fourth *jhāna* has been reached, a strong powerful light called 'the light of wisdom' is produced.

When emerging from this 4th *jhāna*, switch to four elements meditation and see the *kalāpa*s, or minuscule particles. One has to analyse four elements in each *kalāpa*. He proceeds till one reaches and emerges from the 4th *jhāna* before starting *vipassanā*-meditation by means of the four elements method. A shortcut to reach stream-entry is possible, starting with the practice of four elements meditation in a systematic way. The *vipassanā samādhi* one can reach is nearly the same as access concentration. This alternative is said to be based on the *Visuddhimagga*.

— The *Ānāpānasati*-Sutta (MN 118) is relevant to Pa Auk's method to train mindfulness of breathing. However, we cannot trace the attainments of 'the light of wisdom' and 'seeing *kalāpa*s' in MN 118. It remains unexplained how the *Ānāpānasati-Sutta* leads to the 4th *jhāna*. Although one develops the factors of awakening 'inner calm' and 'concentration' during the training of MN 118, not all *jhāna* factors are mentioned in that *sutta*.

In this method, Pa Auk proceeds till one reaches and emerges from the 4th *jhāna* before starting *vipassanā*-meditation by means of the four great elements method. Four elements meditation is taught for instance in the *Mahā-Rāhulovāda-Sutta* (MN 62), as part of a method for development of mindfulness of breathing.[45] Following the exercises of MN 62 trains 'seeing impermanence', leading to giving up the idea 'I am', which means that two typical insight knowledges are reached. So this *sutta* approaches Pa Auk's method, but it does not mention the *kalāpa*s. Besides, MN 62 comprises practices Pa Auk does not refer to, such as the 'four immeasurables', and meditation on what is ugly to counter negative tendencies.

3.1.13 Ledi Sayādaw taught knowledge relevant for insight

Vipassanā-meditation means acquisition of insight by contemplation of impermanence, ill, and no-soul, in Ledi Sayādaw's system. The process concerns arising and ceasing of the four great elements and noting the changes of consciousness. When one discerns impermanence, one can acquire insight knowledge by contemplating no-soul as well. Ledi Sayādaw referred to a *sutta* addressed to Meghiya to argue that impermanence has to be discerned to acquire the insight 'no-soul'.

The four grades of the transcendental path should be developed. When one obtains complete knowledge of ill (*dukkha*), this implies the destruction of lust and conceit. Subtle lust and ill-will are dispelled in the third path. The *jhāna*s have a limited role according to Ledi Sayādaw, as they only temporarily suppress the defilements.

— According to Ledi Sayādaw, one first has to develop the insight into impermanence and then in not-self by means of the four great elements method. This might refer to *sutta* MN 62. However, the transcendental path and thereby complete knowledge of *dukkha* are not part of *sutta* MN 62.

It would have been clearer if the sentence 'the eradication of defilements at the moment of attaining the paths (*magga*) of emancipation' cited above in par. 2.1.13 would have read: the eradication of <u>some</u> defilements at the moment of attaining the paths

[45] Other *sutta*s teaching meditation on the four elements are the *Mahā-Hatthipadopama-Sutta* (MN 28) and the *Dīghanakha-Sutta* (MN 74).

(*magga*) of emancipation.[46] Ledi Sayādaw seems to imply this according to his statement that 'the fourth path dispels the defilements which were left un-dispelled by the lower paths'. Subtle lust and ill-will are dispelled in the third path. The final dispelling of defilements concerns desire for birth in the fine-material-realm, the immaterial-realm, conceit, restlessness, and ignorance.

Ledi Sayādaw referred to 'Meghiya' to support the order of the insights in impermanence and in not-self. Indeed in the *sutta*s addressed to Meghiya (AN 9.3-IV, 356, and *Udāna* iv.1) the thought of impermanence serves to uproot the conceit "I am."

Furthermore, these latter two *sutta*s also teach 'wisdom as to the way of growth and decay, with Ariyan penetration concerning the way to the utter destruction of ill' in the AN redaction[47], respectively 'insight leading to rise and setting' which are 'leading to the destruction of *dukkha*' in the Ud version. So these texts seem to lead to sufficient insight to destroy suffering. However, Ledi Sayādaw seems to disagree, as he wrote that the four grades of the transcendental path have to be developed to obtain complete knowledge of ill, without discussing the Meghiya *sutta*s on this point.

3.1.14 Acharn Mun developed *samatha-vipassanā*

The higher stages of Acharn Mun's method are forms of *vipassanā* practice to develop wisdom and to uproot defilements. Concentrate on breathing in and out until attainment concentration is reached. Then contemplate the repulsive nature of the parts of the body. After reaching access concentration (*upacara samādhi*), the elements method is essential in this practice.

The result is a form of *vipassanā,* clear insight that both knows and sees things for what they actually are which is called '*yathabhūtañāṇa-dassana vipassanā*'. The final *vipassanā*-meditation requires analysis of things as impermanent and suffering and investigation of all things as non-self, until the mind is made to converge. Then the clear insight leading to emergence arises.

---

46 The 'defilements' are often called the ten fetters-*saṁyojana* in the *sutta*s. See Bodhi 2009 (1995): 42 f. for further explanations.

47 The PTS translation of AN 9.3 refers in n. 3 for this text to the first *sutta* of the Nines.

— We can find much of Acharn Mun's practice in the *Mahā-Rāhulovāda-Sutta* (MN 62), which contains the elements method, contemplation of the parts of the body, and attention to breathing with development of concentration. However, the order of awareness of the breath and the elements method is reversed in Acharn Mun's method. The contemplation of the parts of the body in MN 62 does not stress the repulsiveness as in DN 22 or MN 10, but developing the insight that they are not self by analysing the body parts according to their elements.

3.1.15 Brasington teaches insight practice after concentration

Brasington's approach to *vipassanā* practice begins with developing *sīla*, and then suppression of the hindrances by concentration. He teaches to follow the *Sāmaññaphala-Sutta* (DN 2) to at least access concentration. However, higher levels of concentration make insight practice more efficient.

Finally, Brasington teaches insight practice by inserting the 21 *Satipaṭṭhāna-Sutta* practices after the *jhānas*. The insight that has to be developed is real knowledge and vision. Brasington tells us that an alternative way is offered in the *Ānāpānisati-Sutta,* as he understands the last four steps of this *sutta* as insight practices that go to enlightenment.

— DN 2 offers a method to develop *sīla*, and suppression of the hindrances by concentration up to the first *jhāna.* It seems much easier to distinguish the 21 practices Brasington refers to in the *Mahā-Satipaṭṭhāna-Sutta* than in the *Satipaṭṭhāna-Sutta.* So his method may refer to DN 22. Insight in impermanence by contemplation of arising and passing away, and understanding of suffering have been taught in that *sutta* as well. These are insight knowledges, which may be called real knowledge and vision. Although the usual group of insights also contains seeing not-self that is not explicit in DN 22.

As explained above in Chapter 2, Sujato (2001: 58) links the foundations of mindfulness with the 'this is not-the-self' doctrine. Brasington also believes that several of the practices in DN 22 do give insight into not-self. He mentions the Parts of the Body, the 4 Elements, and the 5 *Khandas*.[48] So not-self can be found via DN

[48] Personal communication to me by e-mail, 19.11.2013.

22 as well. In conclusion, Brasington indeed follows a combination of DN 2 and DN 22.

3.1.16 It is possible to analyse a *jhāna* according to Ajahn Thānissaro

According to Ajahn Thānissaro, it is necessary to be concentrated in any one of the *jhānas* from the first one upwards to acquire insight. While you are in any *jhāna* you should analyse and understand the *jhāna* in terms of the five elements of existence (*khandha*s), which you come to see as stressful, not-self, and impermanent. Thereby dispassion and disaffection even for the ease of *jhāna* are developed, till you let go.

Thānissaro sees no clear line between a mindfulness practice, a concentration practice, and an insight practice. He interprets *vipassanā* as a quality of the mind, not something to do. One can analyse a specific *jhāna* while one is in it for understanding stress (*dukkha*) and abandoning the cause of stress. Ajahn Thānissaro refers to MN 52, MN 121; AN 4.126 (II, 130), and AN 9.36 (IV, 422) as bases for his method.[49]

— One can consider in each of the four *jhāna*s that this state is consciously brought about, and thus it is impermanent and has to end, according to Ānanda in MN 52. Even while staying in the first *jhāna* one may in this way destroy the *āsava*s, or continue to consider impermanence in each of the other three *jhāna*s, in the immeasurables and in three *ārupa* meditations. Still, Thānissaro did not explain how one can reason in that way during the second to the fourth *jhāna*, which are without thinking and considering in MN 52 as well. However, according to MN 121 (III, 108), the consideration of impermanence is possible even in the signless *ārupa*, a concentration without any properties. Here, this insight leads to destruction of the taints.

In AN 9.36 (IV, 422) the first person speaker declares that destruction of the taints occurs in dependence of the first *jhāna* or a higher state. In *jhāna* the elements of existence are seen as stressful, not-self, and impermanent. This *sutta* explains that the penetration of final knowledge takes place to the extent that there are

[49] As AN 4.126 (II, 130) concerns kindness and is abbreviated in the PTS translation, analysis in a specific *jhāna* is more evident in AN 4.124 (II, 128).

attainments with perception. In the three lower formless attainments there is no viewing of states comprised by form. Skilled meditators who reach the states of neither-perception-nor-non-perception and the cessation of perception and feeling have to emerge from them first. So, AN 9.36 (IV, 422) takes account of the problems posed by non-perception and the formless attainments.

Ajahn Thānissaro explains a method that is well connected to several *sutta*s, even if some of the ideas in these discourses need further explanation.

3.1.17 The Dhammakāya system

Candasaro Bhikkhu, who developed the Dhammakāya system, stressed the importance of the visualization of forms. The visualization is trained by means of concentration on a clear crystal ball. The development of *vipassanā* by visualization of Buddhas and other human and divine (often Brahma) forms constitutes the essential exercise of this method. Contemplating the spheres is also taught to realize suffering, impermanence and non-self. The highest stage indicated is the eradication of the ten fetters.

— The Dhammakāya method of visualization by means of concentration on a clear crystal ball is related to the *āloka kasiṇa* method of concentration. This is explained in the *Visuddhimagga*. The *Paṭisambhidāmagga* mentions light (*āloka*) and *kasiṇa,* but we did not trace the combination in the *Pāli Tipiṭakaṁ concordance.*

Nor could we trace a Pali canonical source for the development of *vipassanā* by visualization of Buddhas and other human and divine forms. However, Brahmas are often mentioned as visible in *sutta*s, in particular in the *Brahma-Saṁyutta* of the SN, volume I. According to AN 8.64 (IV, 302 ff.), knowledge and vision of the higher *deva*s leads to the realization of being wholly awakened. This may be a source of the Dhammakāya method, but it is hard to see this AN text as a method of meditation.

The practice of contemplation to realize the three characteristics of existence can be connected with *sutta*s such as the *Rāhulovāda-Sutta* (MN 62) and AN 9.3 (IV, 356). The ten fetters are mentioned in SN 45.179 f. (V, 61). To see the eradication of the ten fetters together as the highest stage seems less usual in texts related to *vipassanā*. In descriptions such as MN 6 (I, 34) some fetters are deleted before the highest stage of the Path. But indeed *Arahants* have destroyed them all, as it is one of their qualities (SN 47.4-V, 145).

3.1.18 Kornfield teaches mindfulness and concentration without striving

In Kornfield's method, mindfulness is the key to practice by bare-attention to our experiences. Seeing our own process of body and mind without reacting leads to insight in how things change, in unhappiness, and independence of a permanent self. Practice without striving for anything, until the mind is completely balanced, tranquil, and keenly alert.

After *jhāna* understanding can be deepened. Kornfield uses wisdom resolutions when coming out of *jhāna* such as: 'May a deep insight into anicca arise.' Let go and all suffering will cease. Kornfield's only reference to the canon directs us to one of the last instructions of the Buddha, allegedly "strive on with mindfulness".

— The Buddha's exhortation "strive on with mindfulness" in the context mentioned seems to refer to DN 16 (II, 72 ff.), by combining passages from DN II, 142 and DN II, 156. The first point refers to how a monk should behave when speaking to women: he should take care to be mindful or "Practice mindfulness".[50] The second point declares that 'all conditioned things are of a nature to decay – strive on untiringly.'(Walshe 1987: 270). So the alleged quote seems to offer no support for a special status of mindfulness.

Kornfield's developed his method further, teaching how to use *jhāna* to reach wisdom or *vipassanā* (deep insight) in impermanence.

3.1.19 Momentary concentration and continuous mindfulness suffice for Sharon Salzberg

According to Sharon Salzberg deep insight can be reached by mindfulness. Salzberg uses the term *vipassanā*-meditation, but we traced no definition. However, her statement that momentary concentration and continuous mindfulness provide a platform for a deep insight seems to explain the

[50] Walshe 1987: 264 translates: "Practice mindfulness".

method. The insight gained concerns *anicca, dukkha, and anattā.* Momentary concentration is sufficient in Salzberg's training method. Undistorted moment-to-moment awareness constitutes a moment of liberation. She does not mention canonical sources for her approach.

— Salzberg seems to equate vipassanā-meditation and mindfulness. It is difficult to consider 'a moment of liberation' as the final step to awakening. Salzberg does not mention canonical sources for her approach, and there is no obvious *sutta* connection which comes to mind. Still, we cannot exclude the possibility that this method is connected to a *sutta*, as one who is 'liberated by insight' is known in the *Kīṭāgiri-Sutta* (MN 70-I, 477 f.).

3.1.20 U Ba Khin taught sweeping through the body

According to U Ba Khin, virtue and (preferably) access concentration by awareness of the in-and-out breath must be developed first. Then U Ba Khin gives instruction for *vipassanā*-meditation. To practice the latter, the meditator sweeps the attention through the body, from head to feet and back. The purpose is to experience first matter and then sensations as change. By this introspection the meditator begins to realize that the body and mind are built of minute particles (*kalāpa*s) that are in constant change.

If someone knows, experiences, and understands the nature of impermanence, then suffering and egolessness appear as well. The characteristics of wisdom or insight are right aspiration and right understanding. Finally, by continued practice, passion or anger cease, suffering is extinguished and one is an *Arahant*. Canonical references are to *ānāpāna* for concentration, the final exhortation of DN 16, and several aspects of the noble eightfold Path.

— The abbreviated noble eightfold path in three states can be found in *sutta*s DN 2, 4, 8, and 10. Wisdom is the third. "Right aspiration" and "right understanding" are the first two points of the eightfold Path. U Ba Khin did not explain in our source how the final state -Wisdom- and the first two steps on the path are the same.

The final exhortation by the Buddha in DN 16 (II, 156) may be translated as: "all conditioned things are impermanent – strive on continuously." This fits the concept of impermanence, which is central for U Ba Khin among the characteristics of existence.

However, we did not trace sweeping through the body to experience changing *kalāpa*s in a discourse. It is not mentioned in the index of the late canonical text *Paṭisambhidāmagga* either. *Kalāpa*s just means 'a bunch' in the *Pāli Tipiṭakaṁ concordance*, or *kalāpa* is translated with 'group' according to the Pali-English glossary of the *Abhidhammattha Sangaha.*

3.1.21 Goenka's detailed explanation of sweeping

Goenka (1995: 69) summarizes the process as follows: 'If one develops wisdom and starts observing objectively, the process of multiplication [of *saṅkhārā*] stops and the process of eradication begins.' *Vipassanā-bhāvanā* is a step-by-step method to develop insight. After training to observe bare respiration, the body must be investigated in a very detailed way without reacting. The instruction given for 'sweeping' is that attention should be fixed on small sections of the body, until you feel a sensation.

The changes of all processes in our body and mind also teach that there is no real, unchanging self. Examine pain that arises as if it were someone else's pain, again without reacting. Furthermore, Goenka explains the chain of dependent arising. One must understand that all suffering in life arises because of reactions to liking and disliking, leading to desire and aversion.

— Goenka developed his method from U Ba Khin's, by giving less attention to metaphysical sensations (seeing flashes of light and *kalāpas*), and he offers a more detailed explanation of the sweeping method. Furthermore, he explains the process of how sensations and avoiding reactions to these lead to insight in impermanence, suffering, and no real self.

Goenka does not offer references to specific *sutta*s, but he may have adapted the first exercises regarding attention to the breath and the body of MN 118[51] and MN 10. Dependent arising of the *Vinaya*'s 'second sermon' is also recognisable. Hart, who wrote under supervision of Goenka, refers to DN 16 (II, 123) "The mind imbued with wisdom becomes completely free from the corruptions". Hart has also mentioned MN 118; *Udāna* I.x and VIII.i. The

[51] Hart (1987: 138) mentions the practice of *ānāpāna-sati* as part of Goenka's system.

latter two have made points not directly related to *vipassanā*-meditation.

Table 1 In this table the teachings of 19th-21st century teachers have been ordered according to the most relevant sutta they mentioned, or the sutta we see as related. The latter suttas are marked with 'RvO'.

Teacher or source	**Concept *vipassanā*-meditation**	**Method of *vipassanā*-meditation**	**Which insight**
1 Ajahn Chah	From clear comprehension wisdom will arise.	Continue to develop the mind to see that states of mind are impermanent, unsatisfactory, and not a permanent self.	Finally we understand the four Truths.
2 Bhikkhu Mettavīhari	Insight into the real essence of existence.	Observe the 4 foundations of mindfulness. Practice sixteen *ñāṇas*. Develop insight during 4th-12th *ñāṇas*.	Seeing easily the passing away of *nāma-rūpa* without worldly consciousness.
3 Luangpor Teaan	Liberating knowledge (*paññā*).	Dynamic meditation leads to awareness. *Sati* leads to liberating knowledge.	Total awareness of body and mind in 2nd and 3rd foundations of mindfulness.
4 Venerable Hiran	*Sati* with the intent of insight.	Contemplating the inside of the body.	To see impermanence and *dukkha* and *anattā*.
5 Boonkanjanaram	Mind development through insight is seeing mind and matter as impermanent, suffering and non-self.	Observe each position of the body; and change with right understanding to cure suffering.	*Vipassanā* insight realizes *dukkha-sacca* and *samudaya-sacca* (12th *ñanā*)

Final step to awakening	**Role calm or concentration for insight.**	**Canonical sources**
Enlightenment is attained by letting go.	Calmness meditation for a peaceful and happy mind. However, this should be seen with wisdom as not lasting. No absorption.	Mindfulness, RvO: see *Mahā-SatipaṭṭhānaSutta* (DN 22) because Truths are elaborated.
In the 14th stage of *ñāṇa.*		RvO: see *Satipaṭṭhāna-Sutta* (MN 10).
Arising -extinguishing of the mind.	*Samathi* is important, as well as the 4 Noble Truths.	RvO: see DN 22.
		Sīlā, DN 22.
Right Understanding (*sammā-diṭṭhi*) of the four noble Truths.	Momentary concentration is sufficient.	MN10; DN 22; *Kāyagatāsati-Sutta* (MN 119) (and Vis).

Teacher or source	Concept *vipassanā*-meditation	Method of *vipassanā*-meditation	Which insight
6 Dhiravamsa	Full awareness in every moment of living, without labelling.	Know what arises and passes away in the body and consciousness.	Impermanence; dissatisfactory nature, and voidness.
7 Flickstein	Develop right view.	Exercises of DN 22 & the seven stages of purification.	Intuitive awareness of the meaning of the four Truths.
8 Feldman	Insight.	Includes all 4 foundations of mindfulness; or *Ānāpānasati*	Into the impermanence, the selfless nature, and the suffering of changing experiences.
9 Mahāsi Sayādaw	Develop steadfast insight.	Quietly noting the rising and falling of the abdomen during breathing, leading to growing insight.	Insight that the *khandhas* are *anicca*, *dukkha* and *anattā*. Knowledge of equanimity about formations.
10 Buddhadasa Bhikkhu	Mindfulness of breathing.	The breath is followed at the tip of the nose. Is the breath refined or unrefined?	Continuous contemplating the lack of control, impermanence, non-self of the five elements of existence.
11 Bhikkhu Gunaratana	Concentration together with mindfulness.	Develop attention to the breath to become attentive.	Seeing reality.
12 Pa Auk Sayādaw	Seeing clearly ultimate materiality.	1) Train the awareness of the breath. 2) Develop through 4th *jhāna*. 3) Switch to four-elements- meditation.	Analyse four elements in each small particle (*kalāpa*) that one sees when emerging from 4th *jhāna*.

Final step to awakening	**Role calm or concentration for insight**	**Canonical sources**
Insight leading to the destruction of any clinging.	Has no role for insight.	MN 10.
Idem.	Access or momentary concentration.	DN 22; MN 24; (and Vis).
	Momentary concentration on any object that arises is sufficient. Or intention before access or 1st *jhāna*.	MN 10; or *ĀnāpānisatiSutta* (MN 118).
The insight that the psycho-physical factors are *anicca*, *dukkha* and *anattā* (stream enterer or *Arahant*?).	Concentration is not specified but develops by awareness.	DN 22, especially attention to breathing. RvO: see MN 118.
Getting rid of the defilements makes a noble one.	Concentration below level of first *jhāna*.	Attention to breathing. RvO: see MN 118.
Experience of the three characteristics of existence.	Only during concentration at the level of *jhana* you can see reality.	Attention to breathing. RvO: see MN 118, but *jhāna*?
Stream-entry is the highest stage mentioned.	Mindfulness of breathing as *samatha* practice. The 4th *jhāna* is desirable as basis for *vipassanā*.	MN 118. Development of 4 *jhāna*s. Four-elements- meditation. RvO: see MN 28; MN 62.

Teacher or source	Concept *vipassanā*-meditation	Method of *vipassanā*-meditation	Which insight
13 Ledi Sayādaw	Insight.	Acquisition of insight by contemplation of impermanence, ill, and no-soul.	Insight knowledge in contemplating impermanence, ill, and no-soul. Knowledge of ill is destruction of lust and conceit.
14 Acharn Mun	Clear insight that knows and sees things for what they actually are.	Analysis of all things as impermanent, suffering and non-self.	Continue this investigation until the mind is made to converge.
15 Brasington	Insight practice. Last 4 steps of MN 118.	Develop *sīla* and suppress the hindrances by concentration, thereafter insight practice.	Real knowledge and vision.
16 Ajahn Thānissaro	Insight practice.	No clear line between a mind-fulness practice, a concentration practice, and an insight practice.	Understand the elements of existence as *anicca*, *dukkha* and *anattā*.
17 Vijja Dhammakāya	Realisation of the 'Three Characteristics of Things'.	Constant observation and visualization of Buddhas and other human and divine forms.	Realisation of suffering, impermanence and non-self.

Final step to awakening	**Role calm or concentration for insight**	**Canonical Sources**
Knowledge in the fourth path dispels the last defilements.	The *jhāna*s have a limited role to temporarily suppress defilements.	Arising and ceasing of the four great elements. RvO: MN 28; MN 62. Noting the changes of consciousness.
The clear insight leading to emergence.	First access concentration (*upacara samadhi*) is necessary.	The elements method. RvO: MN 28; MN 62; besides in brief DN 22 and MN 10.
Reaching insight.	Minimum level is access, but higher levels of concentration make insight practice more efficient. But not while in *jhāna.*	Follow *Sāmañña-phala-Sutta* (DN 2) and knowledge and vision by DN 22 practice. Or by the last 4 steps of MN 118.
Dispassion and disaffection even for the ease of *jhāna* till you let go.	Analyse any *jhāna* while one is in it, to understand stress and abandon its cause.	On the role of *jhāna*: AN 4.126, AN 9.36, MN 52, MN 121.
The eradication of the ten fetters.	Visualization of the crystal ball is related to the *āloka kasiṇa.*	*Sutta* not indicated. RvO: on *āloka kasiṇa* see *Vis.*

Teacher or source	Concept *vipassanā*-meditation	Method of *vipassanā*-meditation	Which insight
18 Kornfield	Attention to mind-body process leads to insight.	Develop mindfulness without reacting, and concentration without much striving.	Deep insight into what we really are: *anicca* etc. Besides compassion for all beings.
19 Salzberg	Deep insight.	Momentary concentration and continuous mindfulness provide a platform for a deep insight.	In *anicca, dukkha, and anattā.*
20 U Ba Khin	Mindfulness of the process of moment-to-moment change.	Sweeping the attention through the body, from head to feet vv. to experience first matter and then sensations as change.	Internal particles (*kalāpas*) are in constant change. If one knows, experiences and understands the nature of imper-manence, suffering and egolessness appear.
21 Goenka	Observe sensations.	Attention to the breath and sweeping the body, section by section.	Avoiding reactions to sensations lead to insight in suffering, non-self and impermanence. Equanimity.

Final step to awakening	Role calm or concentration for insight	Canonical Sources
Practice until the mind is completely balanced, tranquil, and keenly alert. Let go.	Wisdom resolutions when coming out of *jhāna* can deepen insight.	DN 16 (I, 156).
The insight gained offers 'a moment of liberation'. (-RvO: probably not awakening).	Momentary concentration is sufficient.	
The aim is right understanding. Passion or anger cease, suffering is extinguished.	Preferably access concentration must be developed before *vipassanā*-meditation.	Short quote from DN 16.
When *saṅkhārā* are eradicated freedom from misery is reached.	Awareness from moment to moment.	DN 16 (II, 123). RvO: see MN 118 and MN 10; Vin 'second sermon'.

3.2 Analysis of methods by scholar-monks

After a brief analysis of the ideas of the scholar-monks as put forward in Chapter 2.2, we comment on the relationship between their methods and the content of the *suttas* they referred to.

3.2.1 Soma Thera explains a gradual path

According to Soma Thera, seeing things according to impermanence etc. is insight (*vipassanā*), which is another name for wisdom. Soma Thera refers to MN 70 (I, 479 f.) for the gradual path to liberating insight. He teaches development of virtue and the need for (at least) the first *jhāna* to separate from the five hindrances (*nivarāna*) that hinder the development of insight (DN 2-I, 71, 73; AN 4.199-II, 211). Of the first *jhāna* it is said that it is the escape from sensuality (MN 36-I, 246 and AN 10.1 f.-V, 1 f.). Virtue, control of the sense-doors, awareness and *jhāna* are the conditions for the development of *vipassanā*.[52]

Serenity is produced in *suttas* DN 22 and MN 10 through mindfulness of breathing (also in MN 118), although according to Soma Thera: 'both discourses on the foundations of mindfulness lay more stress on the development of insight'. Elsewhere Soma Thera even implies that the four *jhānas* are necessary because right concentration, *sammā-samādhi*, has been defined as the four *jhānas* and not anything less (for example DN 22-II, 313).

Study and reflection on the *Dhamma* together with mindfulness and full awareness are necessary to develop wisdom by contemplation. One develops wisdom in the next four purifications following the *Rathavinīta Sutta* (MN 24-I, 148-50). According to Soma Thera, referring to AN 8.19 (IV, 201), full sanctity is reached when someone has fulfilled wisdom.

— Soma Thera offered a method for the attainment of wisdom, referring to canonical sources. However, Soma Thera's argument for the gradual path is not so strong, as the steps in the gradual system of MN 70 (I, 479 f.) differ from his own system. In particular *jhāna* is not mentioned in this *sutta*. The main steps in the part of that

[52] According to Soma Thera (1961: 355-7), the sense-doors must be controlled, and then mindfulness to clean the mind and full awareness of all activities must be developed before the first *jhāna* is possible.

sutta he referred to are hearing the doctrine, examining it, investigating the nature of things, penetrating with wisdom the highest truth and realising it by one's mental body.

AN 10, 1 f.(V, 1 f.) mentions concentration as necessary for release by knowing and seeing, but does not specify that only the first *jhāna* is required. On the contrary, AN 4.198 (II, 210 f.) seems quite explicit that one attains the four *jhāna*s and then directs the mind to knowledge of the *āsavas* and the four Truths.

Furthermore, Soma Thera is not quite convincing when he equated the method taught in the noble eightfold Path to following the order of the seven purifications (MN 24 (I, 148-50). Although it may be that he referred to the summary of the Path in three categories, which agrees with that order. Besides, one can discuss whether the type of calm of the *Ānāpānasati-Sutta* equals the first *jhāna*, as only two *jhāna* factors are mentioned in that *sutta.*[53] So we disagree that MN 118 can be used as indication of the necessity of at least the first *jhāna*. According to AN 8.19 (IV, 201) there is an unspecified gradual training, so Soma Thera needed commentarial sources to explain this means first virtue, then concentration and after that wisdom. *Sutta*s DN 2 and MN 107 may be better sources for this explanation. So the method of the venerable Soma Thera seems defensible, but other *sutta*s than he mentions may offer better support.

3.2.2 Experience the three characteristics of existence

According to Nyanaponika Thera the purpose of the method is insight by unshakable personal experience of the three characteristics of existence. He explains mindfulness by bare attention to rise and fall of the abdomen, and also teaches the impermanence of the body by means of the *Mahā-Satipaṭṭhāna-Sutta* (DN 22) and through the Burmese method. An alternative is the method for mindfulness of breathing (*Ānāpānasati*), in which one distinguishes in a single breath the beginning, middle and end. According to Nyanaponika, access concentration (*upacāra-samādhi*) is the minimum necessary for insight.

53 See Bhikkhu Gunaratana's ideas who made this observation already, as mentioned in sections 2.1.11 and 3.1.11 above.

— Nyanaponika Thera offers clear descriptions of three methods of training that may lead to *vipassanā,* the real experience of the three characteristics of existence. He reminds us that tranquillity or *jhāna* combined with insight training is more frequent in the Buddhist scriptures than bare insight. DN 22 is an example.

But SN 35.70 (IV, 41 ff.) and SN 35.152 (IV, 138 ff.) are said to instruct insight that can lead to holiness without *jhāna.* However, in Nyanaponika's translation, the first teaching only leads to awareness of desires, or their absence, at a certain instance. In SN 35.152 the same method may lead to deliverance. Nyanaponika also admits that rising and falling of the abdomen is not explicitly found in the *sutta*s, but it may be seen as an object of touch or a "sense base". So his canonical foundation of bare attention to the movement of the abdomen is not strong.

The alternative method for mindfulness of breathing is distinct from bare mindfulness, as one instructs oneself during the observations. The taints are only referred to by a quote of SN 47.50 (V, 189 f.); cultivation of mindfulness can destroy them.

3.2.3 The numerical discourses of the Buddha

Bhikkhu Bodhi bases his detailed description of the process to develop wisdom on ample references to *sutta*s from the *Aṅguttara-Nikāya*, one of five collections of teachings. The first stage is the training in higher virtue for monks, the second concerns the development of tranquillity, and the third explains the systematic training to develop wisdom, called *vipassanā-bhāvanā*. This phase of the process begins with mindful attention to the body; then the arising and passing away of the five elements of existence has to be distinguished. That practice leads to the insight into impermanence. Insight into the characteristic of impermanence leads to insight into suffering and in this is not my self. Then revulsion for the elements of existence arises, which, by focussing on *Nibbāna* can be turned into the destruction of lust and craving, craving for existence and ignorance. Thereby liberation by wisdom has been reached.

— Bhikkhu Bodhi offers an almost complete method to liberation by wisdom. He calls this training *vipassanā-bhāvanā*, developing the mind to wisdom by means of thought or meditation. That inclusive term seems more fitting than meditation.

However, Bodhi does not make it totally clear which level of concentration is necessary for success in developing wisdom. We quoted in 2.2.2: 'After mastering the fourth jhāna three pathways open up before the meditator.' The third of these three pathways is the next stage of the process to develop wisdom. From which we tentatively conclude that the fourth *jhāna* is needed to reach wisdom following Bodhi's system.

Bodhi (1999: 27) wrote as well: 'Thus a meditator intent on following the path to its consummation first masters the practice of concentration to a degree sufficient to make the mind calm and unified.' This unclear aspect of his otherwise systematic approach may be justified by differences between AN 9.36 (IV, 422 ff.), which declares that destruction of the taints requires at least the first *jhāna*, and AN 4.41 (II, 44 ff.) where contemplation of rise and fall leads to sufficient concentration to destroy the taints. We will analyze the references Bhikkhu Bodhi has offered in Chapter four, because much detail is involved.

3.2.4 Liberating insight needs *samādhi* according to Bhikkhu Sujato

According to Sujato, *vipassanā* refers to investigation into the nature of reality as experience. Sujato argues that we may summarize the development of insight according to the refrain of MN 10 as contemplation of the inside of the body, explained in MN 118 as: the in-and-out breaths are a certain body. Then, remaining with the body, the principles of origination and dissolution are contemplated (seconded by SN 47.42)[54], establishing mindfulness only as far as necessary for knowledge (AN 6.64 details the kinds of knowledge obtainable by *satipaṭṭhāna*).[55]

Views connected with former times and dependencies on views connected with times to come should be overcome by *satipaṭṭhāna* (DN 29-III, 141). Such views have to be vanquished because they concern an unchanging Self, and as these views are not conductive to the Dhamma.

Furthermore, Sujato stresses the point that *samatha* must be developed in balance with *vipassanā* (AN 2.3.10;[56] Dhp 372), and practice of both has to be gradual. The final steps are the release of heart and the release

[54] PTS: SN XLVII, III, V, ii (V, 184).
[55] =AN III, 418.
[56] =AN I, 61.

by understanding. The release of heart is due to the fading away of lust, anger, and delusion by right *samādhi* explained as the four *jhānas* (DN 22; MN 141; SN 45.8).[57] The release of heart has to be combined with either the release by understanding of reality due to the fading away of ignorance (AN 2.3.10-I, 61), or by understanding, with direct knowledge that lust, anger, and delusion have been permanently uprooted (AN 10.20; SN 52.6, and SN 52.11–24).[58] Elsewhere in the *suttas*, the first *jhāna* is shown to be the minimum necessary prerequisite for *arahant*-ship (MN 64; AN 9.36-IV, 422 ff.).

— Bhikkhu Sujato's work gives the impression that it has been well researched.

However, Sujato uses the refrain of MN 10 as a frame for explaining *vipassanā* practice, while at the same time expressing doubts about it as the refrain varies considerably between the different renderings of *satipaṭṭhāna*. Why would he do that? May be it is just a simplified organisation for teaching purposes.

Sujato has stated that DN 22 is nothing more than a late expansion of MN 10 and the four Noble Truths were taken from MN 141. Contrary to this point, Sujato indicated for instance DN 22 as a source for 'right *samādhi*'.

Sutta AN 2.3.10-I, 61 apparently teaches that the development of both *samatha* and *vipassanā* are equally important. Development of *vipassanā* leads to understanding. Development of understanding leads to the fading away of ignorance and release by understanding.

Sujato's references SN 52.6 and SN 52.11–24 explain the results of cultivating the 'four arisings of mindfulness'. But only SN 52.24 (LII, VIII, II, xiv-V, 305 f.) states that this can lead to destruction of the *āsavas*:

"...I attain and abide in that heart's release, that release by insight which is freed from the āsavas." Furthermore, SN 52.7 (LII, VIII, I, vii-V, 300) teaches that cultivation of the four *satipaṭṭhānas* conduces to the destruction of craving.

---

57 PTS: SN XLV, I, I, viii (V, 10).

58 PTS: AN 10.20 (V, 29ff.); SN LII, VIII, I, vi (V, 299) and SN LII, VIII, II, xi-xiv (V, 303 ff.).

3.2.5 Anālayo shows that insight can be developed in two ways

According to Bhikkhu Anālayo, real insight needs to be based on a sound moral foundation and development of tranquility to reach mastery over the mind, and leaving sensuality behind (MN 43-I, 294; AN 2.3.10-I, 61). Anālayo describes two sequences leading to insight based on discourses, although he notes that in the early discourses *vipassanā* stands predominantly for insight as a quality to be developed and not for a specific meditation technique.

Once morality and tranquility are developed, the first method continues with observing different aspects of breathing. One has to develop penetrative awareness of impermanence and see properly that this is unsatisfactory (Th 1117). So according to MN 22 (I, 138) because of these qualities, 'what is impermanent, unsatisfactory and subject to change' is not mine, nor myself. This is a guided method of meditation according to Anālayo for the development of liberating insight. *Sutta* AN 5.72 (III, 85 f.) combines these insights with the perception of eradication of the defilements in the mind and perception of dispassion. Dispassion is the proximate cause for liberation.

As a second method, Anālayo describes certain practices of the *Satipaṭṭhāna Sutta* supporting the development of insight. One sees that life depends on the breath, and that 'my body' consists of the four elements. Observing changing feelings develops insight into impermanence and non-self as well (MN 140-III, 244; DN 15-II, 67). Insight into impermanence of the five constituents (*khandhas*) destroys clinging to self and often features as a last step to liberation (DN 14-II, 35; DN 33-III, 223; SN 12.23-II, 29; SN 18.22-II, 253; AN 4.41-II, 45 and AN 8.2-IV, 153).

Insight in the four noble Truths equals full insight into the dependent arising of *dukkha* and its cessation (MN 4-I, 23). According to MN 56 (I, 380), full insight into the dependent arising of *dukkha* and its cessation leads to stream entry, and in MN 4 (I, 23) the result is full awakening. Right concentration as a factor of the noble eightfold Path frequently means the four absorptions. However, according to several discourses the first absorption suffices to attain awakening, when no attachment is left (MN 52-I, 350; MN 64-I, 435; AN 9.36-IV, 422 and AN 11.17-V, 343).

— Anālayo offers two approaches to *vipassanā*, and how this quality may be developed according to *sutta*s. The investigation-of-phenomena awakening factor may be relevant for the development of insight, however, in *sutta* MN 118 (III, 85) this is one of seven factors of awakening to be fulfilled. According to Anālayo, insight into impermanence of the five elements of existence (*khandha*s) often features as a last step to liberation. However, in the PTS translation of SN 12.23 (II, 29), it goes together with liberation, which is caused by passionlessness. Besides, according to SN 18.22 (II, 253), seeing any aggregate as not mine is right insight and liberation.

According to MN 56 (I, 380), the hearing of the four noble Truths indeed leads to the *Dhamma*-vision "whatever is of the nature to uprise, all that is of the nature to stop." However, there seems to be a discrepancy between the fruits of MN 56 and MN 4, as the knowledge of the four Truths in MN 56 (I, 380) refers to stream-entry and according to MN 4 (I, 23) this insight leads to full awakening. There it leads as well to insight in and destruction of the taints. *Sutta* AN 3.88 (I, 235) calls the understanding of the four Truths the training in the higher insight, and combined with AN 3.89 (I, 235 f.) these support MN 4 (I, 23).[59]

Finally, according to AN 9.36 (IV, 422) as well as MN 64 (I, 435), Buddha teaches that the first *jhāna* may be sufficient to reach the destruction of the taints, when there is insight in the impermanence of this concentration and if there is no attachment left. In MN 52 (I, 350) and AN 11.17-V, 343), Ānanda teaches the same.

3.3 Conclusions on the comparison of recent *Vipassanā* teachings with Pali *sutta*s

Bhikkhu Anālayo, Bhikkhu Sujato, Acharn Mun, Brasington and Ajahn Thanissaro offer methods of *vipassanā* practice, which seem both complete and in general well founded on the texts of *sutta*s. They and other teachers mention a number of *sutta*s which will be investigated in more detail in the next chapter. Bhikkhu Bodhi describes a process to liberation by wisdom on the basis of many *sutta*s from the *Aṅguttara-Nikāya.*

[59] AN 3.89 declares that training in the higher insight leads to destroying the *āsavas* and the monk comes to know the heart's release, the release by insight.

The minimum level of concentration needed to reach clear insight is the first *jhāna* (Thānissaro, Sujato, Anālayo), the *jhāna*s (Brasington), or access concentration (Mun). In this respect Soma Thera and Bhikkhu Bodhi are less clear, this might be because the AN teaches several levels of concentration as sufficient.

Other teachers often teach one step of the eightfold path, namely *sati*, in some cases on a basis of morality. Still, simple systems may offer good results as well. For example mindfulness directed to the body (taught at Boonkanjanaram) may lead to clear comprehension and abandonment of ignorance according to AN 1.21.48 (I, 43ff.).

According to many teachers and scholar-monks *vipassanā*-meditation requires analysis of the four [great] elements earth, water, fire and air of a 'person' as impermanent, as suffering, and as non-self. This can be based on *sutta*s such as MN 28 (I, 185 ff.), MN 62 (I, 421 ff.), MN 74 (I, 500); AN 5.72 (III, 85 f.); and Th 1117. *Sutta*s MN 74 and AN 5.72 combine these thoughts with the thoughts of renunciation and of dispassion. Thorough development of these thoughts has as fruits: liberation or mind emancipation and insight-emancipation.

Sutta AN 3.88 (I, 235) calls the understanding of the four Truths the training in the higher insight, and this may be combined with AN 3.89 (I, 235 f.) which states that the training in the higher insight destroys the taints. These *sutta*s support the teaching in MN 4 (I, 23) that such understanding of the four Truths and of the taints lead to knowledge of release by insight. Dispassion may be the proximate cause for liberation.

It seems fitting to call the systematic training to develop insight towards wisdom "*vipassanā-bhāvanā*", as Bhikkhu Bodhi does. That term seems more apt than meditation as it includes thought, analysis, contemplation, meditation, and other training practice. In Part II of this research we will apply this idea, translating it by the "development of insight", as Nyanaponika translated *vipassanā-bhāvanā* sometimes.[60] "Insight" is chosen to stay close to the literal meaning of *vipassanā.*

Some teachings often included in the *vipassanā* practices of today seem to lack a canonical foundation. Methods including the development of the sixteen *ñāṇa*s follow a Theravāda tradition which is later than the *sutta*s, according to Anālayo and Warder. Dry insight, without the support of mental calm, is a commentarial idea, according to Gunaratana. Anālayo as well did not trace that idea in the early discourses.

---

[60] Nyanaponika 1975 (1962): 63, but in his glossary he translated *vipassanā* (*-bhāvanā*) as insight meditation'.

The three methods which Nyanaponika explains supposedly lead to insight without reaching *jhāna*, although he admits the canonical foundation of bare attention to the movement of the abdomen is not strong. Flickstein acknowledges that the part of his method in which he combines the seven stages of purification mentioned in MN 24 with their elaboration in the *Visuddhimagga* and with the exercises of DN 22, has no foundation in the canon.

3.4 Conclusions on the working hypotheses

In Chapter 2 we developed three working hypotheses, based on the methods of the twenty-one teachers of insight meditation as summarized there. We confront these with the arguments of scholar-monks and the most relevant Pali *sutta*s, to see whether they can be refuted or corroborated in that way.

Regarding our first working hypothesis, 'Practices which only teach attention to the breath only teach one step of the eightfold Path, namely *sati'*, several scholar-monks have argued in line with it that more is needed than a practice which only teaches attention to the breath to develop the eightfold Path. In particular morality and concentration to at least the first *jhāna* are necessary.

However, contrary to the first working hypothesis mindfulness of breathing (MN 118) can be employed to develop tranquillity and insight. So this method is not limited to *sati*. For tranquillity a method teaches just mentally knowing the presence of the breath. This may be based on the following interpretation of the third phase of the practice in MN 118 (III, 82): train to experience the in-and-out breaths as a certain body. Anyway, MN 118 (III, 82-3) has tranquilizing the activity of body and thought as exercises, and further on in the text the monk develops the links in awakening "tranquillity" and "concentration".

Second working hypothesis: 'a) The level of concentration needed to reach clear insight is not indicated in an unequivocal way in the *sutta*s.' This is supported in the research of these scholar-monks, although most agree that according to the *sutta*s the first *jhāna* is the minimum necessary to reach insight.

As stated in working hypothesis 2 b) 'the idea that momentary concentration is sufficient for release, is contrary to right concentration'. Sources that make that clear are DN 22, MN 141, and SN 45.8. It is also contrary to several *suttas* which require at least the first *jhāna* to win insight and destruction of the taints (MN 64-I, 435; AN 9.36-IV, 422). Still, the level of tranquillity needed before beginning the development of insight is undetermined (AN 4.170-II, 157).

Third working hypothesis: 'The final step to awakening remains uncertain.' Indeed, two alternatives are taught thus:

First, insight into the impermanence of the five elements of existence of a 'person' features in many discourses as a last step to liberation by destroying the taints (DN 14-II, 35; DN 33-III, 223; SN 18.22-II, 253; AN 4.41-II, 44 ff. and AN 8.2-IV 153). According to SN 18.22 (II, 253) this insight erodes the foundation of clinging to a self. In DN 14 (II, 35) insight into the impermanence of the five elements of existence, ends clinging to anything.

Second, insight into the four noble Truths as in the last exercises in the *Mahā-Satipaṭṭhāna-Sutta* implies full insight into the dependent arising of *dukkha* and its cessation. So it may form the highest insight. However, the fruit is uncertain as according to MN 56 (I, 380) understanding the four noble Truths leads to stream-entry and in MN 4 (I, 23) to full awakening. AN 3.88 (I, 235) combined with AN 3.89 (I, 235 f.), as well as MN 112 support MN 4 (I, 23).

The scholar T. Vetter calls the knowledge of the four noble Truths 'liberating insight'. This insight destroys the different kinds of desire and ignorance, and is supposed to be finally liberating. This combination of desire(s) and ignorance came to be called *āsava*, which can be translated as cankers, imperfections etc. (Vetter 1988: 29-30).

PART II

Chapter 4

Insight according to *suttas* in the *Vinaya* and *Sutta-Piṭaka*

Now we switch the focus from the teachers and scholar-monks to the canonical sources on how to attain insight, in particular to the *suttas* of the *Sutta-Piṭaka* (mainly of the first four Nikāyas) and a few famous teachings in the *Vinaya*. Which *suttas* offer methods of *vipassanā*-meditation or rather *vipassanā-bhāvanā*? And which methods are well supported by the *suttas*?

It seems useful to require at least two sources that have to some extent independently developed. We suppose that different traditions of reciters restrict late cross influences. So we choose in this chapter the following criteria: at least explained in *suttas* of two Pali *Nikāyas*, or in one *Nikāya* and the Pali *Vinaya*.

4.1 Insight in the *Vinaya (Mahāvagga)*

According to the *Dhammacakka-pavattana-Sutta* (the 'First Sermon') in the *Vinaya* and in SN LVI, XII, II, i (V, 420 ff.), the vision, the knowledge and the insight in the attainment of being liberated are essential.[61] We summarize L. Schmithausen's (1981: 207 f.) ideas on the *Vinaya* discourse. Liberation included the practice of the Path and the vanishing of the taint of craving.

However, the Buddha only was assured of this liberation by the knowledge that this cause of suffering has been abandoned and that the Path has been practised. Thus the teaching on the Buddha's enlightenment may have been the starting point for the idea of insight into the noble Truths as a condition for awakening.

[61] *Vinaya Mahāvagga* 6.37 ff.-I, 10 ff. and Schmithausen 1981: 207.

The so called 'second-teaching'

In the *Vinaya* a more complex method for insight is taught as well, the 'second-teaching'. The five constituents or elements of existence (*khandhas*) have to be seen as 'non-self' (*anattā*), firstly because if they were the self, they would not lead to affliction and one would have ones wishes as to body etc. fulfilled.

The second argument is that the *khandha*s must be seen as impermanent, because of this they are suffering (*dukkha*) and so should be regarded by means of right wisdom as not my self (*Vinaya*, *Mahāvagga* I, 6.37 ff.- I, 13f.). Seeing thus the instructed disciple disregards the five *khandha*s. "[D]isregarding he is dispassionate; through dispassion he is freed;" and he knows that he is freed. According to the *Vinaya*, the minds of the first five monks were freed from the cankers (taints) and became perfected just by hearing this discourse (Vin. 6.46-7). So according to Vetter (1988: 35-6), this teaching does not require *jhāna*.[62] He calls this method the path of discriminating insight (Vetter 1988: xxxiv; 35).

Several *sutta*s support the 'second-teaching': SN 22.59 (III, 66) explains why the constituents are *anattā*, with the same arguments as the second-teaching as related in the *Vinaya*. MN 22 (I, 138-9), MN 109 (III, 18 f.) and SN 12.70 (II, 124 f.) teach that the body and the other constituents of a 'person' have to be seen as impermanent, suffering and subject to change, so they should be regarded as not my self.

Seeing the five elements of existence thus by means of wisdom, apparently denotes *vipassanā* according to Tse-fu Kuan (2008: 59). This method leads to freedom in the same way as taught in the *Vinaya* 6.37-46 (I, 13-4). *Sutta* MN 22 does not require *jhāna* for liberation either.

Three *sutta*s in the *Aṅguttara Nikāya* (6.98 ff.- III, 441 f.) even teach that it is impossible to realize the fruits of stream-winning to *arahant*-ship, without seeing all conditioned things (*saṅkhārā*) as impermanent, unsatisfactory, and all things (*dhammā*) as not-self (Tse-fu Kuan 2008: 59).

— In conclusion, these teachings of the *Vinaya* suggest two ways to insight. The first includes the practice of the eightfold Path that culminates in the reaching of the four *jhāna*s, the ending of (the taint of) craving and the knowledge that these objectives have been accomplished.

[62] However, we should consider that these monks had been ascetics for a long time already.

The second method teaches the insights that the five elements of existence or constituents are non-self, impermanent, and suffering. We call these the three typical *vipassanā* insights. Seeing these leads one to disregard the five elements of existence, and thereby one is freed from passion. Hearing this discourse led the first disciples to freedom from the *āsava*s (taints, cankers).

4.2 Selection and discussion of *suttas*

4.2.1 *Sutta*s selected on the basis of references in Chapters 2 and 3

- *Sutta*s similar to the *Vinaya* methods to insight

Sutta SN LVI, XII, II, i (V, 420 ff.) corroborates the 'First Sermon' in the *Vinaya* redaction, and specifically the knowledge that the Path has been practised:

> "At the thought: This Aryan truth about the practice leading to the ceasing of Ill has been cultivated, concerning things unlearnt before there arose in me vision, insight, understanding: there arose in me wisdom, there arose in me light."

This quote is F.L. Woodward's (1956: 359) translation of:

> *"Idam dukkhanirodhagāminī paṭipadā ariyasaccan ti me bhikkhave pubbe ananussutesu dhammesu cakkhum udapādi ñāṇam udapādi paññā udapādi vijjā udapādi āloko udapādi‖"* (SN V, 422)

So here insight into the four noble Truths is directly linked to, and a condition for the knowledge of being awakened. And SN LVI, XII, II, ii (V, 424-5) even suggests that "there arose in me vision, insight, understanding, wisdom, there arose in me light." is the awakening.

Three *sutta*s were mentioned above as related to the method of the 'second-teaching' in the *Vinaya*: SN 22.59 (III, 66); MN 109, and also MN 22. *Sutta* SN 22.59 (III, 66) explains why the constituents are *anattā*, *anicca* and thus *dukkha* in the same two ways as in that *Vinaya* text. According to MN 109 (III, 18-9) an instructed, well trained pupil sees that the elements of existence are suffering, not my self, and impermanent, and seeing thus leads to disenchantment, becoming dispassionate and liberation.

The Buddha teaches in MN 22 the same insights, with an accent on giving up that what is not my self. Seeing thus, an instructed disciple of the noble ones turns away from the five elements of existence and becomes dispassionate. Becoming passionless he is liberated and the knowledge that he is liberated arises in him (MN 22-I, 138 f.). In these *sutta*s *jhāna* is not mentioned.

The *Chachakka-Sutta* (MN 148) seems related to this method.
This discourse expounds six groups of six dhammas. The Buddha is said to have taught how craving arises. Then he explained the impermanence of all those *dhamma*s and that therefore they cannot be the self. When one succeeds in not holding on to feelings, by abandoning the tendencies to feelings one can arouse true knowledge.

> "Bhikkhus, that one shall here and now make an end to suffering by abandoning the underlying tendency to lust for pleasant feeling, by abandoning the underlying tendency to aversion towards painful feeling, by extirpating the underlying tendency to ignorance in regard to neither –painful- nor pleasant feeling, by abandoning ignorance and arousing true knowledge-this is possible."
>
> (MN 148-III, 286; transl. Bodhi 2009:1135)

That true knowledge can lead to disenchantment, next dispassion arises, and so it is possible to end suffering here and now (MN 148). This discourse concludes that when the Buddha taught this discourse, by not clinging the minds of sixty monks were liberated from the taints.

- *Sutta*s on mindfulness

The *Kāyagatāsati-Sutta* (MN 119) and AN I.21.1 ff. (I, 43 ff.) are *sutta*s which specifically teach the value of mindfulness directed to the body. A similar training is part of *sutta*s DN 22 and MN 10. Furthermore, MN 119 teaches the four *jhāna*s. The final steps in MN 119 are destruction of the taints, realization of the taintless liberation of the mind, and liberation by insight.

According to AN I.21.1 ff. (I, 43 ff.), mindfulness directed to the body leads to clear comprehension and abandonment of ignorance and realization of the deathless. However, in this text or in MN 119 the three typical *vipassanā* insights are not developed. These are not even mentioned among the benefits of mindfulness directed to the body in MN 119, and AN I.21.1 ff. (I, 43 ff.) only makes explicit that 'the delusion of self is given up'. Nyanaponika and Bhikkhu Bodhi (1999: 39, n. 24) commented on AN I.21.1 ff. (I, 43 ff.), thus: 'The great stress laid on contemplation of the body derives from the fact that meditative comprehension of the impermanent, painful and selfless nature of bodily processes forms the indispensible basis for a corresponding comprehension of mental processes; and it is only the comprehension of both that will lead to liberating insight and the noble path.'

Because the understanding of the impermanent, painful and selfless nature is implicit, these *sutta*s are incomplete although a good basis. So we conclude that MN 119 and AN I.21.1 ff. (I, 43 ff.) do not teach how to reach all *vipassanā* insights and they do not offer a complete method of *vipassanā-bhāvanā*.

The core subject of the *Ānāpānasati-Sutta* (MN 118) is the attention to breathing that has to be trained in sixteen phases. Specific exercises to observe impermanence, detachment, stopping and casting away constitute the last four phases of that section (MN 118 (III, 83). These may be regarded as practices specifically aimed at insight.[63] Casting away can be letting go of attachments by insight. Up to this point a very similar meditation system has been taught in the *Vinaya* (chapter Defeat, vol. 1, III, 1, 3-III, 70-1). It is interesting that this method has been called "*ānāpāna-satisamādhi*" in that *Vinaya* text itself, so apparently this training concerns concentration with mindfulness or both concentration and mindfulness. However, insight is not mentioned as a result.

According to MN 118, when this attention to breathing is seriously developed, the four foundations of mindfulness are realized as well. Similar insight exercises as in the last four of the above sixteen phases to observe impermanence etc. have been included in this part also.

Then the seven factors for awakening arise one by one, which include tranquillity. When the body is tranquil, thought is concentrated and the monk develops concentration. Looking with proper care at this, he develops equanimity. The level of concentration is not specified in MN 118. Still, full development of the seven factors for awakening seems to be sufficient for liberation:

[63] Breet and Janssen 2005, MN vol. 3: 172 n. 113.

"Monks, when the seven links in awakening are developed thus, are made much of thus, they bring to fulfilment freedom through knowledge." (MN 118-III, 88)

So this *sutta* seems to lead to awakening. However, MN 118 does not explicitly explain how to develop insight in *dukkha* and *anattā*.

The *Mahāsatipaṭṭhāna-Sutta* (DN 22) offers a more complex method than the *suttas* investigated above. One trains first in mindfulness of breathing, and the following body meditations include a review of the four elements which constitute the body.

In between these exercises there is a refrain which may be considered as relevant for insight. A part of the refrain indicates: "He abides contemplating arising phenomena in the body, he abides contemplating vanishing phenomena in the body" (DN 22-II, 293, Walshe 1987: 336). This exercise to understand the principles of origination and dissolution is seconded by MN 10 and SN XLVII, III, V, ii (V, 184). Furthermore, the refrain stipulates that the mindfulness of the body is established in him just to the extent necessary for bare knowledge and continuous mindfulness.

Similar contemplations as about the body are taught for feelings, the mind and mind objects. The repeated awareness of rising and vanishing may lead to insight in impermanence, though the term is not mentioned in DN 22.

This *Dīgha Nikāya* version of the *sutta* explains the four Noble Truths extensively, including a detailed explanation of many aspects of suffering. Pondering this explanation can lead to a deep knowledge of suffering, which may be called insight. Insight in the four noble Truths equals full insight into the dependent arising and cessation not only of *dukkha* but also of the three taints (MN 4-I, 23). The fourth Truth is the way of practice that leads to the cessation of *dukkha*, and the last subject of this eightfold Path is usually called right concentration. Its explanation starts and ends as follows:

"Here a monk, detached from sense-desires, detached from unwholesome mental states, enters and remains in the first *jhāna*, which is with thinking and pondering, born of detachment, filled with delight and joy."
"And, having given up pleasure and pain, and with the disappearance of former gladness and sadness, he enters and remains in the fourth *jhāna,* which is beyond pleasure and pain, and purified by equanimity

and mindfulness. This is called Right Concentration. And that, monks is called the way of practice leading to the cessation of suffering." (DN 22-II, 313, transl. Walshe 1987: 349)

So, here right concentration means development of all four *jhāna*s in the context of the eightfold Path (idem MN 141-III, 252; SN XLV, I, I, viii-V, 10). The final exercise is again the refrain including:

> "He abides contemplating arising phenomena in mind-objects, he abides contemplating vanishing phenomena in mind-objects, he abides contemplating both arising and vanishing phenomena in mind-objects." (DN 22-II, 314, Walshe 1987: 349)

But the mindfulness of the mind-objects should not go beyond the knowledge and awareness of their presence according to the refrain, as the last two sentences of it and the exercises read:

> "And he abides detached, not grasping at anything in the world. And that, monks, is how a monk abides contemplating mind-objects in respect of the Four Noble Truths." (DN 22-II, 314, Walshe 1987: 349)

Furthermore, the *vipassanā* insights in impermanence and in suffering are developed, though not explicitly mentioned by these names. *Sutta* DN 22 does conclude that a profound knowledge (*aññā*) is the cause of becoming an Arahant or non-returner.[64] However, this *sutta* DN 22 does not train or name the insight in "this is not my self", and the destruction of the taints. Furthermore, we did not find the concepts "development of *vipassanā*" or "*vipassanā*-meditation" in the translations used.

An alternative for the practice taught in DN 22 is the combination of the *Satipaṭṭhāna-Sutta* (MN 10-I, 55 ff.) with MN 141. The reason is that in MN 10 the four noble Truths are just mentioned, but not explained, while in MN 141 these truths are explained in detail. The latter discourse develops insight in impermanence as well (MN 141 -III, 270 ff.).

Following Anālayo's (2008: 12-4) classification, from the perspective of the *Mahāsatipaṭṭhāna-Sutta* (DN 22) we consider the *Majjhima-Nikāya Satipaṭṭhāna-Sutta* both to be a parallel (in the case of the part that does correspond to the other version) and not a parallel (in the case of the part

---

[64] T.W. and C.A.F. Rhys Davids mention in DN 22 that *aññā* is an epithet of *arahant*ship (PTS: 1910); Walshe 1987: 350 translates *aññā* directly with 'Arahantship'.

that does not correspond). So we would interpret MN 10 as a 'partial parallel' to DN 22.

- Meditation on the elements

The elements meditation has been taught in the *Mahā-Rāhulovāda-Sutta* (MN 62). These exercises describe five elements of the body and the external world (earth, water, fire, wind, and space). Then according to MN 62 (I, 422) one has to see these as they really are, with right insight "This is not mine, this am I not, this is not my self."

Thereafter the four meditations on loving kindness, compassion, altruistic joy and equanimity are taught. Added to these are meditations on whatever is ugly to give up passion, and on awareness of impermanence to end the false idea 'I am'. Finally in MN 62, the Buddha explains a method for the development of mindfulness of breathing. During these exercises he trains concentration and during the final breathing exercise he trains to see impermanence, disintegration, ceasing and relinquishment. The result is awareness of the last breath at death. Two insights, this is not my self and impermanence, are thoroughly trained in MN 62, but *dukkha* is not mentioned.

However, MN 61 is complementary, as Rāhula is also the pupil therein. *Sutta* MN 61 instructs Rāhula to consider at each bodily, verbal and mental action whether it leads to more suffering for oneself or others. If so one should abstain, if possible. The result is purification of all actions.

So together these two *sutta*s offer a thorough training to obtain the insights in the characteristics of existence, but the results are awareness and purification of all actions. We consider this outcome as limited, because these teachings do not lead to liberating insight, awakening or *Nibbāna.*

Sutta MN 140 (III, 240-5) considers six elements including consciousness and besides the feelings, leading to insight in this is not my self and impermanence of feelings. The highest insight refers here to the knowledge related to the destruction of all suffering.

- *Sutta*s stressing the importance of *jhāna* for insight

Many *sutta*s, in particular in the *Majjhima-Nikāya*, teach a way to reach liberation by means of the four *jhāna*s and then one has to direct the mind to the three knowledges: of former abodes, of rise and fall of beings, and of the taints. The final one of these aims at the destruction of the taints or cankers. The results are the understanding of the four Truths, understanding of the cankers and knowledge of freedom.

Tse-fu Kuan (2008: 57) explains this process thus: 'This practice culminates in the fourth *jhāna*, which is characterized as *upekkhā-sati-pārisuddhi*, a state of pure equanimity and mindfulness. The fourth *jhāna* provides an optimal emotional state and cognitive capability, which prepare the mind for the ultimate spiritual goal, and thereby enable one to attain liberation through developing the three gnoses (*vijjā*) or knowledges (*ñāṇa*), as stated in many texts.' Kuan refers to MN 4, MN 27, MN 39 and MN 51, which indeed describe the process we mentioned above.

According to *sutta* MN 64 (I, 435-7), the Buddha taught that destruction of the taints can occur in dependence of the first *jhāna* or a higher meditative state, and in AN 9.36 (IV, 421 ff.) the first person speaker declares the same. These *sutta*s teach that, while in *jhāna,* the elements of existence should be seen as impermanent, as suffering [etc.], as not-self. Contemplation of these characteristics of existence (im-permanence, unsatisfactoriness, and this is not my self) belong to *vipassanā*-meditation, the development of wisdom (Tse-fu Kuan 2008: 78).

Abiding in *jhāna* one focuses on the deathless element thus: "This is the peaceful, this is the sublime, that is, the stilling of all formations, the relinquishing of all attachments, the destruction of craving, dispassion, cessation, *Nibbāna*." (MN 64).[65] "Standing upon that, he attains the destruction of the taints. But if he does not attain the destruction of the taints", than he attains final *Nibbāna* elsewhere, "without ever returning from that world."[66] That means he becomes a non-returner. So the destruction of the taints implies a higher achievement than becoming a non-returner, which can only mean becoming an *Arahant*.

Furthermore, *sutta* AN 9.36 (IV, 421 ff.) explains that the penetration of final knowledge takes place to the extent that there are attainments with perception. In conclusion, MN 64 and AN 9.36 (IV, 421 ff.) teach important principles, but are mainly concerned with concentration, as the part on the method to develop insight is only brief. Still, training to see impermanence, unsatisfactoriness and this is not the self belong to *vipassanā-bhāvanā,* the development of insight. Ānanda taught a similar way to liberation according to MN 52 (I, 350). According to that discourse, attaining

[65] MN 64, transl. Ñāṇamoli and Bodhi 1995: 540-1. Tse-fu Kuan 2008: 78 points to a similar description as the content of wisdom in SN V 226.

[66] Sutta MN 64-I, 435-7, transl. Ñāṇamoli and Bodhi 1995: 540-1.

Nibbāna in a *jhāna* is possible, if one understands that *jhāna* as a conditioned and thus impermanent state.

AN 4.198 (AN II, 211) is quite explicit that after abandoning the five hindrances, one attains the four *jhāna*s and then directs the mind to knowledge of how to destroy the *āsava*s (taints). One first comes to know the four Truths. Thereafter, one comes to know the *āsava*s, the arising of *āsava*s, the ending of the *āsava*s, and finally he knows and sees thus:

> "This is the practice going to the ending of the *āsava*s. In him, thus knowing, thus seeing, his heart is released from the *āsava* of sense-desire; his heart is released from the *āsava* of becoming; his heart is released from the *āsava* of ignorance. By release comes the knowledge: I am released." AN 4.198 (AN II, 211)

However, as we noted already, according to AN 9.36 (IV, 421 ff.) destruction of the taints occurs in dependence of the first *jhāna* or a higher state. In *jhāna* a monk may see the elements of existence as impermanent, as suffering, as ill etc., as non-self. His mind turns away from those states and towards *Nibbāna*. So the requirement of the concentration that has to be reached may be less stringent than AN 4.198 (AN II, 211) taught, when two conditions are fulfilled: he should be steadfast in contemplating *Nibbāna* and there should not be attachment to the *Dhamma*. *Sutta* MN 64 corroborates that the first *jhāna* may be sufficient to reach *Arahant*-ship by destruction of the taints.

- A gradual method to develop *sīla, jhāna* and destruction of the taints

The *Sāmaññaphala-Sutta* (DN 2) explains a gradual method to develop *sīla*, restraint of the senses, and then one concentrates on keeping mindfulness established to suppress the hindrances. When he is detached from the five hindrances, he enters and remains in the first *jhāna*. According to Brasington (in Shankman 2008: 160), who uses DN 2 to start his training-method, access concentration is sufficient for insight practice. However, Brasington prefers to switch to the 21 *Satipaṭṭhāna*-excercises after reaching the *jhānas*.

However, DN 2 continues with the development of concentration to reach the fourth *jhāna*. Only then the meditator "inclines his mind to knowing and seeing" (DN 2-I, 76, Walshe 1987: 104). He knows the dependent origination, suffering and impermanence of the body and that his consciousness depends on that body. Thereafter he develops super-normal powers and knowledges such as seeing beings passing away and arising.

In the last exercise, he with mind concentrated "applies and directs his mind to the destruction of the corruptions". Then he first knows the four noble Truths (these are mentioned but not trained here). DN 2 continues:

> "And he knows as it really is: 'These are the corruptions', 'This is the origin of the corruptions', 'This is the cessation of the corruptions', 'This is the path leading to the cessation of the corruptions.' And through his knowing and seeing his mind is delivered from the corruption of sense-desire, from the corruption of becoming, from the corruption of ignorance, and the knowledge arises in him: 'This is deliverance!', and he knows: 'Birth is finished,'"
>
> (DN 2-I, 83, Walshe 1987: 107-8)[67]

In conclusion, DN 2 offers an almost complete method to develop insight, in which only "this is not my self" is implicit. Still, it is remarkable that this practice was taught to king Ajātasattu, who had killed his father and only confesses this and becomes a lay follower of the Buddha at the very end of DN 2.

- The seven stages of purification

The seven stages of purification of the *Rathavinīta-Sutta* (MN 24) have been elaborated in the *Visuddhimagga. Sutta* MN 24 describes a discussion between two monks, in which the stages of purity of moral behaviour figure till "purity arising from knowledge and insight is of purpose as far as utter nibbāna, without attachment." (MN 24-I, 150)

Because this process is not elaborated in the form of exercises in MN 24, this sutta only offers a frame and no method. Therefore, Flickstein correlates these stages with the exercises of DN 22 in his method. Flickstein (2003: 21) notes that the seven stages of purification of the *Rathavinīta-Sutta* (MN 24) are not elaborated in the canon, and we have not traced them there either.

---

[67] The 'corruptions' of sense-desire, of becoming, and of ignorance are according to (for example) AN 6.63 and AN 9.36 the *āsava*s, elsewhere translated as fluxes, taints or cankers.

- The development of insight according to the *Aṅguttara-Nikāya*

The whole method of *vipassanā-bhāvanā* may be developed on the basis of *sutta*s in the *Aṅguttara-Nikāya*, according to Bhikkhu Bodhi's introduction in the AN anthology by Nyanaponika and Bhikkhu Bodhi (N and B 1999). Insight knowledge has to be developed by systematic training, called *vipassanā-bhāvanā*.[68] *Sutta*s AN 2.3.10-I, 61 and AN 4.94-II, 93 f. both underline the need for tranquillity of mind as well. Then, with a quiet mind a meditator attends mindfully to the body (N and B *sutta* 11=AN I.21.1 ff. (I, 43 ff.).

When mindfulness becomes clearer he or she learns to distinguish the five elements of existence (*khandha*s) as they arise and pass away (N and B *sutta* 59=AN 4.41-II, 44 ff.). According to that *sutta*, this practice leads to the insight into impermanence and indirectly into suffering and this is not my self. Because the elements of existence are unstable and constantly disintegrating, one realizes these are really concealed forms of suffering (*dukkha*). 'And whatever is impermanent and suffering cannot be identified as a truly existent self.' (Bodhi in N and B 1999: 27)

Impermanence, suffering and non-self are the three universal characteristics of existence (N and B *sutta* 48=AN 3.134-I, 286). Because these three are inextricably interwoven, insight into one leads to insight into the others (N and B *sutta* 142 §§ 5-7=AN 7.46-IV, 46 ff.). To contemplate the three characteristics deeply is the essence of insight meditation (Bodhi in N and B 1999: 27; N and B *sutta*s 138-40=AN 6.102-4-III, 443 f.). The deep knowledge of these three characteristics leads the mind to turn away from the five elements of existence (*khandha*s) with revulsion.

The mind focuses on *Nibbāna*, because that is perceived as the only true security and peace. Revulsion changes into 'dispassion, the fading away of lust and craving, and dispassion in turn culminates in liberation (*vimutti*), the mind's release from all fetters.' (Bodhi in N and B 1999: 27-8)[69] The Buddhist path culminates in the destruction of the taints (*āsava*s) of the mind, which means destroying "sensual craving, craving for existence and ignorance" (N and B *sutta* 131 §4=AN 6.63-III, 410 ff.; N and B *sutta* 181=AN 9.36-IV, 422 ff.). When the taints are totally destroyed 'the

[68] Nyanaponika and Bhikkhu Bodhi 1999 *sutta*s 14=AN 2.3.10-I, 61; and 72=AN 4.94-II, 93 f.

[69] Bodhi refers to N and B *sutta*s 28=AN 6.52-III, 362 ff.; 182=AN 10, 1-V, 1 f., and 183=AN 10, 2-V, 2 ff.

disciple enters upon "the taintless liberation of the mind, liberation by wisdom, having realized it for himself by direct knowledge" (Bhikkhu Bodhi in N and B 1999: 28). This disciple has become an *Arahant*, a worthy one.

— However, many of the teachings referred to in the above section are more complicated than the point used by Bodhi, as the following examples show. *Sutta* AN 4.41 (II, 44 ff.) is a method to develop four kinds of concentration and not only leads to insight into impermanence. *Sutta* AN 4.94 (II, 93 ff.) ends with: "Therein, monks, the person who gains both internal tranquillity of mind and the higher wisdom of insight into things should establish himself in these wholesome states and make a further effort for the destruction of the taints." So tranquillity of mind is one of the aspects.

Sutta AN 7.46 (IV, 46) explains that the perception of impermanence offers a basis to develop first insight into suffering, and then perception of this is not my self may be developed from insight into suffering. So there is no automatic process by which insight into one leads to insight into the others.

The *sutta*s quoted by Bodhi do not state that revulsion changes into dispassion. However, other texts make that connection thus: according to AN 7.46 (IV, 46), deep knowledge of the three characteristics of existence leads to aversion to the five elements of existence or to equanimity towards these. *Sutta*s AN 6.52 (III, 362 ff.); AN 10, 1 (V, 1 f.) and AN 10, 2 (V, 2 ff.) refer to revulsion and dispassion together.

After an exposition on the taints, AN 6.63 (III, 362 ff.) teaches *kamma* and its cessation; and suffering and its cessation. For all three subjects (taints, *kamma* and suffering) the noble eightfold Path is called the way to their cessation. So AN 6.63 (III, 362 ff.) does not prove that the destruction of the taints is the culmination of the Buddhist path.

However, AN 9.36 (IV, 422 ff.) indeed implies that attainment of the destruction of the taints means becoming an *Arahant*, because when attachment to the *Dhamma* prevents the destruction of the taints one becomes a non-returner. A non-returner is just one stage below an *Arahant*. Still AN 10.90 (V, 174 f.) is ambiguous on what happens after the destruction of the taints, as this *sutta* teaches that many powers are "made to grow" in a monk who has destroyed the cankers. Among these powers is "the Ariyan eightfold Way" before "he comes to know: destroyed in me are the cankers."

We conclude that the AN teachings Bhikkhu Bodhi has referred to, offer much information on which aspects to develop towards insight. If one wants to construct a training method from this information, it leads to a complicated package, on which many remarks may be formulated.

- Training of impermanence as a method leading to insight

One of the methods to develop insight consists in observing different aspects of the process of breathing (MN 118). First penetrative awareness of the impermanent nature of reality must be developed (AN 7.46-IV, 51; Th 1091: *vipassaṁ*). Comprehensive insight into impermanence then needs to lead on to insight into unsatisfactoriness and into not my self or emptiness (Th 1117). That which is impermanent because of that quality is unsatisfactory.

Furthermore, according to *sutta* MN 22 (I, 138), it is not appropriate to see 'what is impermanent, unsatisfactory and subject to change as "this is mine, this I am, this is my self". Turning away from the five elements of existence, one is freed from passion, by being free from passion one is liberated and the knowledge that one is freed arises (MN 22-I, 139). This constitutes a method to develop liberating insight (Anālayo 2010: 85).

Another method to gain insight in impermanence is contemplation of the changing nature of feelings (DN 22; MN 10; MN 140 (III, 244); and more theoretical in DN 15 (DN II, 66). Dwelling in contemplation of the rise and fall of the five elements of existence leads to freedom from the corruptions (taints) (DN 14-DN II, 35; DN 33-DN III, 223; AN 4.41 (AN II, 45). Furthermore, in AN 8.2 (IV, 153) and SN 48.10 (V, 199) this contemplation of rise and fall is conductive to getting wisdom.

This wisdom of rise and fall leads to the understanding of the four Truths (SN V, 199). It may also be enough to destroy the taints, as it is stated in a text that in him who knows and sees the uprising and passing away of the five elements of existence, the intoxicants (taints) are extinct (SN 12.23-II, 29).

Impermanence has to be discerned to acquire the insight 'no-soul', according to the *suttas* AN 9.3 (IV, 356) and *Udāna* 4.1, both addressing

Meghiya. Both these *sutta*s contain the teaching on the order of these insights in a similar way, so we just quote *Udāna* 4.1:

> "For, for the one perceiving impermanence, perception of not-self becomes anchored, (whilst) the one perceiving not-self reaches the uprooting of the conceit of "I am", (reaches) nibbāna in these seen conditions". (*Udāna* 4.1)

So insight in impermanence leads to insight in not-self, which destroys vanity. Besides, *Udāna* 4.1 as well teaches that "insight leading to rise and setting" is "leading to the destruction of *dukkha*." Discourse AN 9.3 (IV, 356) seems somewhat different on this point, stating that "wisdom as to the way of growth and decay, with Ariyan penetration concerning the way to the utter destruction of ill." So in the latter *sutta* wisdom seems to offer insight into the Path, which still may have to be followed, while according to the *Udāna* version insight in rise and fall leads to liberation from suffering.

In MN 146 (III, 271 ff.), a monk teaches first insight in the three characteristics of existence (impermanence, suffering, perception of this is not my self) and then the seven factors of awakening to nuns. The results of thorough development of these are said to be as follows:

> "by the destruction of the cankers, having here and now realised by one's own super-knowledge the freedom of mind and the freedom through intuitive wisdom that are cankerless, entering on them and abides therein." (MN 146-III, 275)

However, the connections between the three characteristics of existence, the factors of awakening and destroying the taints are not explained in this text.

4.2.1.1 Conclusions: the level of concentration and the type of insight differ

It seems clear that insight needs to be based on a good moral foundation and the development of tranquillity or concentration. According to MN 149 (III, 289); AN 2.3.10 (I, 61) and Dhp 372, *samatha* must be in balance with *vipassanā*. However, both the level of tranquillity or concentration needed before beginning the development of insight and the order of developing these two qualities are undetermined (AN 4.170-II, 157).

Right concentration as a factor of the noble eightfold path frequently means the four absorptions (for example in DN 22; MN 141, and SN XLV, I, I, viii-V, 10). However, according to several discourses the first absorption suffices to attain awakening (MN 52-I, 350; MN 64-I, 435; AN 9.36-IV, 421 ff., and AN 11.17-V, 343).

Tranquillity or concentration has to be combined with one of the following four kinds of insight:

a) The release by insight or understanding of reality due to the fading away of ignorance (AN 2.3.10-I, 61). Understanding reality means insight in the three universal characteristics of existence: impermanence, suffering, and this is not my self (AN 3.134-I, 286; *Vinaya*, *Mahāvagga* I, 6.37-46 (I, 13-4). We call these the three typical *vipassanā* insights. Seeing these leads one to disregard the five elements of existence, and thereby one is freed from passion; or

b) Release by understanding, with direct knowledge that lust, anger, and delusion have been permanently uprooted (AN 10.20-V, 31 f.); or

c) Release by insight which is freed from the *āsava*s. The latter are the taints of craving, becoming, and ignorance (SN LII, VIII, II, xiv-V, 305-6). *Sutta*s MN 64 and AN 9.36 (IV, 422 ff.) as well suggest that destruction of the taints equals becoming an Arahant; or

d) Insight in the four noble Truths and insight into the dependent arising of the taints and their cessation means attainment of liberation (DN 2-I, 83 f. and MN 4-I, 23). According to MN 56 (I, 380) full insight into the dependent arising of *dukkha* and its cessation leads to stream entry, and in MN 4 (I, 23) the result is full awakening. According to MN 140 (III, 245), liberation means insight of the destruction of all suffering.

The 'First Sermon' in the *Vinaya* and SN LVI, XII, II, i (V, 422) both teach that liberation includes the practice of the Path and the vanishing of the taint of craving. However, the Buddha only was assured of this liberation by the knowledge that this cause of suffering has been abandoned and that the Path has been practised. Thus the teaching on the Buddha's enlightenment may have been the starting point for the idea of insight into the noble Truths as a condition for liberation.

The *Vinaya* offers two arguments to understand non-self (*Vinaya, Mahāvagga* 6.37 ff.-I, 13 f.). First argument: the body (or visible form) tends to sickness and we cannot say that we want the body to become thus. The same arguments make clear that we do not control the other elements of existence. Because of our lack of control of the five elements of existence these are impermanent and not as we wish. Therefore they are non-self.

Second argument: that which is impermanent because of that quality is unsatisfactory. According to MN 22 (I, 138), it is not appropriate to see what is impermanent, unsatisfactory and subject to change as "this is mine, this I am, this is my self".

4.2.2 *Sutta*s selected on the basis of indexes of the *Sutta-Piṭaka*

Methods to develop insight or inward vision (*vipassanā-bhāvanā*) involve the strengthening of the faculty of wisdom (*paññā*), according to Bodhi 2010 (1993): 67. We will select *sutta*s where the development of insight and/or wisdom is taught, as far as these *sutta*s were not yet treated above. Therefore the conclusions after each paragraph regard the teachings discussed there, and not in a whole *Nikāya.* We used the indexes of the PTS editions for the MN, AN, and SN and of Walshe's translation for the DN.

4.2.2.1 Insight and wisdom in the *Dīgha-Nikāya*

In the *Dīgha-Nikāya* the word "*vipassanā*", let alone its use in a combination with a method of meditation or development (*bhāvanā*), is rare according to M. Walshe's index of the *Dīgha-Nikāya*. However, several methods related to "*paññāvimutti*" have been expounded. Walshe (1987: 638) translated this term "*paññāvimutti*" with "liberation by Wisdom". As insight and wisdom are both related to liberation by mental development and sometimes used as synonyms, we will also discuss "*paññāvimutti*".

We used Walshe's (1987) translation of the DN for the following section, where a method leading to insight is associated with the name of Prince Vipassī (DN 14-II, 21, 31-5).

Prince Vipassī states he found the *vipassanā* way. His method according to DN 14 concerns conditioned arising and cessation (Walshe 1987:

211-3). The part in which Vipassī states he has found the way to awakening begins with "By the cessation of mind-and-body consciousness ceases," and the final steps in this process of cessation are: "by the cessation of feeling craving ceases; by the cessation of craving clinging ceases; by the cessation of clinging becoming ceases; ... birth ceases; ...suffering ceases." Understanding a chain of what conditions ageing and death, Vipassī thought: "I have found the insight (*vipassanā*) way to enlightenment." (DN 14-II, 34f.)

The thought of "cessation" leads to insight and vision. Interesting is the next contemplation attributed to Vipassī in DN 14-II, 35:

> "And as he remained contemplating the rise and fall of the five aggregates of clinging, before long his mind was freed from the corruptions without remainder."[70]

Thereby he became an Arahant and a Buddha.[71] Here we find a way to destroy the taints, which is moreover associated with a system to develop insight.

If a monk knows all the spheres where beings dwell as they really are, their origin and cessation, their attraction and peril, he is freed without attachment, according to DN 15 (II, 68 ff.). That monk 'is called one who is liberated by wisdom.' (Walshe 1987: 229) Walshe has noted that several of those spheres or 'stations' formally correspond with some of the eight liberations.

These liberations, which are taught next in the same *sutta*, can also lead to liberation by wisdom (DN 15-II, 70 f.) 'The difference is that by the first way these 'stations' are seen through with insight and rejected, whereas by the second way they are used as a means towards liberation.' (Walshe (1987: 566, n. 355) So, these are two more ways to liberation by wisdom.

According to DN 29 (III, 131 f.), the Buddha expounded activities leading to pleasure which bring beneficial results, leading to deliverance through wisdom, thus:

---

[70] "the five aggregates of clinging" are the five elements of existence or constituent parts of an 'individual' (*khandhas*).

[71] Vipassī was a Buddha 91 *kalpas* ago (DN 14).

> "There are, Cunda, these four kinds of life devoted to pleasure which are entirely conductive to disenchantment, to dispassion, to cessation, to tranquillity, to realisation, to enlightenment, to Nibbāna."
> (DN 29-III, 131-2; transl. Walshe 1987: 434)

Then the Buddha taught the four *jhāna*s and the benefits of these states. The four benefits are the four paths from Stream-Winner to attainment of *Arahant*-ship.

> "The fourth is when a monk, by the destruction of the corruptions in this very life has, by his own knowledge and realisation, attained to Arahantship, to the deliverance of heart and through wisdom."
> (DN 29-III, 132)

In this case the *jhāna*s are combined with the destruction of the corruptions (taints) and with deliverance by wisdom.

Sutta DN 33 (III, 270 f.) tells us what liberated by wisdom means:

> 'He understands: "For me greed, hatred and delusion are abandoned, cut off at the root, like a palm tree stump, destroyed and incapable of growing again." (Walshe 1987: 509)

A non-learner (*asekha*) has ten qualities in DN 33, verse 3.3(6), having established the eightfold Path, he has all its factors from right view till right concentration. Furthermore, he has right knowledge (*sammā-ñāṇam*) and right liberation (*sammā-vimutti*) (Walshe 1987: 509 f.).

— We conclude that on the basis of Walshe's index only one *sutta* of the *Dīgha-Nikāya* uses the word "*vipassanā*" in relation to a method. This method emphasizes understanding a cessation process, and thereby an insight way to enlightenment is found. Further contemplating the rise and fall of the five elements of existence of an 'individual', one can free the mind from the taints; thereby one becomes an *Arahant* (DN 14-II, 35).

Two methods are related to higher spheres such as the eight liberations, and these lead to liberation by wisdom (DN 15-II, 69 ff.).

A fourth method combines the *jhāna*s with the destruction of the taints as follows. As a result of the *jhāna*s the monk attains the stage of stream enterer, and by the destruction of the taints the monk may finally reach the attainment of deliverance of heart and by wisdom (DN 29-III, 132). This is interesting as these results are not mentioned in for example DN 22.

The typical insights, namely into impermanence, into unsatisfactoriness and into this is not my self have not been made explicit in these *Dīgha-Nikāya* teachings.

In DN 14 and DN 29 the destruction of the taints and knowing this are the final steps to becoming an *Arahant*.

According to DN 33, liberated by wisdom means understanding that greed, hatred and delusion are abandoned. One has established not only the eightfold Path, but also right knowledge (*sammā-ñāṇa*) and right liberation (*sammā-vimutti*) according to DN 33 (III, 270 f.).

4.2.2.2 Insight and wisdom in the *Majjhima-Nikāya*

We only found two cases of the word "*vipassanā*" related to meditation or development of insight in the index of the PTS edition of the *Majjhima-Nikāya*. Once 'calm and vision' are mentioned, namely in MN 73 (I, 494). In that discourse someone should develop two things: *samatha* and *vipassanā*. Secondly, according to MN 111 (III, 25), Sāriputta had uninterrupted insight (*vipassanā*) during half a month. But these examples offer no instructions or method for the development of insight. Much more often freedom by or through intuitive wisdom (*paññāvimutti*) or freedom through knowledge (*vijjā*) are mentioned.

Right view and right intention are the factors of the Path often associated with insight and so with the development of *vipassanā* (M. Walshe 1987: 25; de Breet and Janssen 2004: 47-49). In the *Majjhima-Nikāya* a *sutta* has been dedicated to right view, namely MN 9. The Buddha taught in MN 117 that right view comes first in relation to right concentration and other factors of the noble eightfold Path. *Sutta* MN 117 explains the inter-relationships of the eight factors of the Path and relates these to right knowledge and deliverance thus:

> "Therein bhikkhus, right view comes first. And how does right view come first? In one of right view, right intention comes into being; in one of right intention, right speech comes into being; in one of right

speech, right action comes into being; in one of right action, right livelihood comes into being; in one of right livelihood, right effort comes into being; in one of right effort, right mindfulness comes into being; in one of right mindfulness, right concentration comes into being; in one of right concentration, right knowledge comes into being; in one of right knowledge, right deliverance comes into being.

Thus, bhikkhus, the path of the disciple in higher training possesses eight factors, the Arahant possesses ten factors."

(MN 117-III, 75 f.; transl. Ñāṇamoli and Bodhi 1995: 938 f.)

So 'first' means here that right view has to be understood and developed first, it does not mean it is the highest. The passage quoted offers a clear order of the development of the factors of the noble eightfold Path, and adds right knowledge (*sammā-ñāṇa*) as the final factor before deliverance. Right knowledge depends on right concentration, the latter should be supported by the seven other factors of the Path and is called "noble right concentration with its supports and its requisites" (MN 117-III, 71).

According to MN 9 many methods can lead to someone having right view, but in all cases the way that leads to the stopping of the problematic aspect is the noble eightfold Path. The last two methods are about ending ignorance and the taints (MN 9-I, 54 f.). Ignorance means not knowing about the four noble Truths. The arising of the taints causes the arising of ignorance. The way to end ignorance is the noble eightfold Path. Seeing through ignorance in this way ends suffering in this life. Then one becomes someone with the right view. Next in MN 9, the same Path is taught about seeing through the taints, their origin from ignorance, the ending of the taints and the same Path stops the taints as well, when all aspects of the Path are perfected. The taints (or cankers) are defined here as sense pleasures, becoming and ignorance. Comprehending the taints and the way to end them thus, he gets rid of attachment, of addiction to shunning, and of the latent view "I am". Knowledge (*vijjā*) ends suffering.

Furthermore, Sāriputta teaches in MN 43 (I, 294) how right view can be developed to deliverance. According to this *sutta,* moral habit, hearing, discussion, calm and vision (insight - *vipassanānuggahītā*) forward right view, in Pali:

"Idh' āvuso *sammādiṭṭhi sīlānuggahītā ca hoti sutānuggahītā ca hoti sākacchānuggahītā ca hoti samathānuggahītā ca hoti vipassanānuggahītā ca hoti.*" (MN 43-I, 294)

So, in the above PTS translation *vipassanā* is rendered with 'vision' instead of insight. But Bodhi (2009: 390) translates "Here, friend, right view is assisted by virtue, learning, discussion, serenity, and insight". The results mentioned in this *sutta* are freedom of mind, "and the fruit of freedom through intuitive wisdom and the advantage of the fruit of freedom through intuitive wisdom." (MN 43-I, 294)

Several *sutta*s may be related to right aspiration (*sammā-saṅkappa*), such as MN 6 (in particular I, 35 f.), MN 73, and MN 120. Monks can realise freedom through wisdom, if they wish. One should fulfil the moral habits, train in the rules of training, be intent on mental tranquillity, and one should not interrupt meditation. Furthermore, one should be endowed with vision and cultivate empty places. By the destruction of the taints, by one's own super-knowledge, here and now freedom of mind and freedom through wisdom can be entered on according to MN 6 (I, 35-6). However, these very general conditions seem insufficient as a method to develop insight.

Sutta MN 73 (I, 496) confirms that someone wishing to reach freedom of mind, the freedom by intuitive wisdom ("*paññāvimutti*"), can achieve this after destruction of the taints. This *sutta* mentions some other conditions: a good base, living solitary, being ardent and energetic.

Sutta MN 120 also offers a teaching on uprising (becoming again) through aspiration. However, MN 120 (III, 103) makes clear that another resolve can conduce to freedom by intuitive wisdom in the present life ("*paññāvimutti*"). These *sutta*s point, in my opinion, to the importance of right aspiration. However, even though some conditions are mentioned, it is hard to see these as complete methods to reach wisdom.

We discussed the release by intuitive wisdom, which destroys the *āsavas*, or is freed from them. The *āsava*s are translated as the taints, corruptions, intoxicants, or sometimes as the cankers. Is the destruction of the taints cause or result? In MN 40 it is a cause, thus:

> "And if one has gone forth from home into homelessness from a noble's family,[72] and by the destruction of the cankers, having here and now realised by one's own super-knowledge freedom of mind, the freedom through intuitive wisdom that are cankerless, entering on them, abides therein-he is a recluse through the destruction of the cankers."
> (MN 40-I, 284)

[72] The same is said of other families.

Here destruction of the cankers is the means to reach freedom by intuitive wisdom, so first it is the cause. It seems self-evident that someone is then 'cankerless'. This order finds support in MN 4, MN 112, MN 119; AN 6.64 (III, 417 ff.), and AN 9.36 (IV, 422 ff.).

When someone develops and cultivates the seven factors of (or for) enlightenment, with the destruction of the cankers this leads to freedom through intuitive wisdom. A monk mentions these links in enlightenment in MN 146 (III, 275), but does not offer a practical method of meditation.

According to Vetter (1988: 36-8), an old source for discriminating insight is the method of MN 74 (I, 499 ff.), in which the body, which consists of four elements, has to be seen as impermanent, suffering etc. and as non-self. Next, feelings have to be seen as impermanent, arisen dependent and liable to cessation or similar predicates. If the disciple sees feelings in this way he gets enough of feelings, and he becomes dispassionate. Then the mind is freed (Bodhi 2009: 606). When Sāriputta heard this, he contemplated it and was freed from the taints without grasping anything anymore.

— So, selection on the basis of the index of the PTS edition of the *Majjhima-Nikāya* rarely links the term "*vipassanā*" with meditation. More often this search leads to the purpose: freedom by wisdom in combination with freedom of heart. Right view and right understanding, by means of the noble eightfold Path, can end ignorance and the taints, according to MN 9 (I, 54-5).

The factors moral habit, hearing, discussion, calm and vision will forward (*vipassanānuggahītā*) right understanding (*sammā-diṭṭhi*). This results in freedom through intuitive wisdom (MN 43-I, 293 f.). A strong resolve combined with several conditions as well can lead to freedom by intuitive wisdom (MN 6-I, 35 f.; MN 73, and MN 120).

The insights into impermanence, unsatisfactoriness and this is not my self are taught in MN 74. One has to see the body and the other elements of existence, which consist of the four elements, as impermanent etc. to get enough of these. It may end the taints and grasping.

4.2.2.3 The development of insight and wisdom in the *Aṅguttara Nikāya*

We searched the *Aṅguttara Nikāya* by means of index of the PTS edition for *vipassanā* and *paññā*. The principle of calm (*samatha*) must be cultivated to abandon lust and *vipassanā* must be cultivated to abandon ignorance according to AN 2.3.10 (I, 61), as we already saw in par. 2.3.4.

*Sutta*s AN 2.17.3 ff. (I, 100) do not distinguish the results of developing calm and insight. In the latter *sutta*s, the cultivation of calm and insight together is necessary for the comprehension of lust, anger, delusion etc. In these *sutta*s no method or process for the cultivation or development of insight is taught, and besides the required level of calm is not specified.

However, AN 4.147 (II, 140) offers a hint of a method, stating that if rightly and each in due time developed, hearing the Dhamma, understanding the Dhamma, calming, and insight (*vipassanā*) gradually lead to destruction of the *āsava*s. So, theoretical knowledge and calm and insight must be gradually developed and "rightly revolved", which probably means contemplated.

Which insight destroys ignorance? The higher insight can mean understanding of the four noble Truths, or destruction of the taints leading to knowledge of the release of the heart, the release by insight. *Sutta* AN 3.88 (I, 235) explains the training in the higher morality, the training in the higher thought, and the training in the higher insight. The "training in the higher insight" (*adhi-paññāsikkhā*) is as follows:

> "Herein a monk understands, as it really is, the meaning of This is ill: This is the arising of Ill: This is the ending of Ill: This is the practice leading to the ending of Ill."
>
> (Translation F.L. Woodward 1960: 214)

So here the insight that has to be trained means a right understanding of the four noble Truths.

However, according to AN 3.89 (I, 235 f.) which is the next *sutta*, the training in the higher insight is explained as:

> "Herein a monk, by destroying the āsavas, himself in this very life comes to know thoroughly the heart's release, the release by insight which is without the āsavas, and having attained it abides therein."
>
> (AN 3.89-I, 235 f.)

Sutta AN 4.5-II, 6 offers a very similar text, changing the release by insight in "the release by wisdom".

There are many references to wisdom (*paññā*) in the AN. According to AN 9.44 (IV, 452 f.) someone is called wisdom-freed (*paññāvimutto*) if one enters and abides in the first concentration or a higher level of concentration and by wisdom understands it.

Paññāvimutti/o is translated in other ways as well: release by insight according to the PTS translation of AN 2.3.10 (I, 61) or release by understanding (Sujato 2001: 27). Tse-fu Kuan (2008: 58) states 'Although *samatha* and *vipassanā* may not have quite the same meaning as concentration and wisdom, there is hardly any doubt that they refer to concentration and wisdom respectively.'

— We would rather suggest on the basis of AN 2.3.10 (I, 61) and MN 43 that the development of insight (*vipassanā*) develops wisdom (*paññā*).

In AN 2.9.1 (I, 83) 'emancipation of insight' is one of a number of conditions without further explanation. Knowledge is a way to release according to AN 10.105 (V, 214):

> "But, monks, when knowledge leads the way, by the attainment of profitable states the sense of shame and self-restraint follow in its train. In one who is swayed by knowledge and has good sense, right view springs up. Right view gives rise to right thinking ... right concentration gives rise to right knowledge, and that to right release."[73]

It is noteworthy that "right knowledge" and "right release" extend the eightfold path into a tenfold way, just as in MN 117.

Sutta AN 10.54 (V, 98 ff.) corroborates that a monk must have both peace of heart (similar to calm) and insight, but that the order may vary. This is in agreement with AN 4.170 (II, 156 f.). The insight in AN 10.54 is called "wisdom of the higher and insight into dhamma", in Pali *adhipaññādhammavipassanāya*, sometimes in the same PTS translation this *paññā* has been rendered by insight. If he is a winner of peace of heart, but did not yet win wisdom and insight, he must try to acquire that.

---

[73] The other steps of the eightfold Path are implied, as the contrary aspects (wrong view etc.) are mentioned before in the same text.

"If, however, on self-examination a monk knows thus: I am a winner of insight of the higher and insight into dhamma, but not of peace of heart in my own self – then he must make an effort to establish the one and acquire the other." AN 10.54 (V, 98 f.)

Once he succeeded in having both qualities, "then he must make an effort to establish just those profitable conditions, and further destroy the cankers." Thus, in AN 10.54 (V, 100) there is no automatic release by insight, but a further effort is necessary for the destruction of the taints. However, this text does not offer much as an instruction on how to develop the two qualities of peace of mind and insight, nor how to destroy the taints.

Sutta AN 4.93 f. (II, 92 ff.) again states that calm and insight are both to be developed. A person who has established mental calm, but not the higher wisdom of insight into things should make an effort to attain the insight (AN 4.93-II, 92). According to the next text AN 4.94 (II, 93 ff.), one has to ask someone who has gained that insight: "How are the activities to be understood? How are the activities to be seen into?"

There are a few other instances of the concept *vipassanā* in the *Aṅguttara- Nikāya.* According to AN 9.4 (IV, 360) a monk having faith, virtue and calm of mind, but who 'cannot obtain by more-wisdom insight into things' (*adhipaññādhammavipassanā*) has to think:

"Would that I might have faith and virtue, obtain calm of mind within and obtain by more-wisdom insight into things." (AN 9.4-IV, 360)

Sutta AN 10.71 (V, 132 f.) offers some instructions on what a monk has to do, if he wishes to reach the taintless release of heart, the release by insight: 'then let him be a fulfiller of the virtues, in his own self given to peace of mind, not rejecting musing, possessed of insight and fostering resort to lonely spots.' 'Musing' is an old word for meditation or contemplation. The requirements are clear, but how to acquire that insight is not explained. The requirements when a monk wishes to reach freedom through insight are similar to those of MN 6 (I, 35 f.).

Besides the instances mentioned of *paññā* in the AN which offer some idea of a last step to wisdom, compounds such as *bhāvitapaññā, suvimuttipaññā, paññāsampanno* are used in contexts which do not explain a method for the development of insight or wisdom.

— The search for *vipassanā* and *paññā* on the basis of the index of the PTS edition of the *Aṅguttara-Nikāya* leads to the following conclusions. According to AN 4.147 (II, 140), theoretical knowledge and calm and insight must be gradually developed and probably contemplated.

AN 10.54 (V, 98 ff.) corroborates that a monk must have both peace of heart and insight, but that the order in which these are developed may vary, just as in AN 4.170 (II, 156). That insight has been called "wisdom of the higher and insight into dhamma", which is a translation of *adhipaññādhammavipassanāya*. A person who has established mental calm, but not the higher wisdom of insight into things should make an effort to attain the insight (AN 4.93--II, 92), or ask someone who has gained insight (AN 4.94-II, 93 ff.).

The English words "higher insight" and "wisdom" are sometimes used in very similar contexts. The training in the higher insight may lead to comprehending the four noble Truths (AN 3.88-I, 235), or release by insight may be reached by the destruction of the *āsava*s (AN 3.89 (I, 235) and AN 4.5 (II, 6).

According to AN 9.44 (IV, 452 f.) someone is called wisdom-freed (*paññāvimutto*) if one enters and abides in the first concentration or a higher level of concentration and by wisdom understands it. In AN 2.3.10 (I, 61) *paññāvimutto* is also translated by release by insight. As methods to develop insight, these texts are not detailed in comparison to some other teachings such as the *Satipaṭṭhāna-Sutta*s.

4.2.2.4 The development of insight and wisdom in the *Saṃyutta-Nikāya*

The index of the PTS edition of the *Saṃyutta-Nikāya* only offers three references to *vipassanā*, but about 30 to *Paññāvimutti/a*. Of the latter we will mention only a few examples.

According to SN XLV, I, I, xi (V, 52), *samatha* and *vipassanā* are the states that are to be cultivated (*bhāvetabbā*) by full comprehension. *Sutta* SN 35.204 (IV, 195) combines *vipassanā* with calm in a parable as a couple of swift messengers, explained as follows: "'Pair of swift messengers,' brother,--this is a name for calm and insight." These came by "the Ariyan Eightfold Path, to wit, right view and the rest ... and right concentration."

So here insight is a result of following the eightfold Path and not of a more specific method. This is corroborated in MN 149 (III, 289).

Alternatives can be found in the SN chapter 43 (IV, 360 ff.), as this chapter briefly mentions many paths to the uncompounded. The latter concept is explained as the destruction of lust, hatred and illusion (SN 43.1-IV, 360). One of those paths consists of calm and insight (*suttas* 2 and 12), however, mindfulness relating to the body, and concentration that is void, signless and aimless, are some of the other paths mentioned there.

The taints (*āsavas*) are enumerated in the usual way in the *Saṃyutta Nikāya* thus:

> "There are three taints, O monks: the taints of sensuality, the taint of desire for renewed existence, and the taint of ignorance.
>
> For eliminating these three taints, O monks, the four Foundations of Mindfulness should be cultivated."
>
> (SN 47.50-V, 189 f.; transl. Nyanaponika 1975 (1962): 146)

So, this text links the (*Mahā*)-*Satipaṭṭhāna-Sutta* to the destruction of the taints.

When the *āsavas* have been destroyed, some SN discourses teach that a monk still has to cultivate and make much of the controlling faculties. There are one till five controlling faculties in the series of discourses in SN XLVIII, IV, V, v ff. (V, 222 ff.), and *paññā* (in the PTS translation 'insight' or 'Ariyan insight') is one of these. If a disciple by cultivating and making much of the controlling faculty of *paññā* has won insight (*paññāvato*), the other controlling faculties are established as well (SN XLVIII, IV, V, v-V, 222).

In these *suttas* the result is *añña*, translated as 'gnosis' and the end of rebirth. The controlling faculty of insight (*paññindriyam*) is reckoned chief for attaining the wisdom that is awakening (*bodhāya*) according to SN XLVIII, IV, VI, iv-v (V, 231-2) and SN XLVIII, IV, VII, x (V, 238 f.).

However, another *sutta* in the same volume of the SN (LV, XI, III, iv-V, 376) gives the impression that the destruction of the taints is sufficient to win release thus:

> "Now by the destruction of the āsavas, in this very life, by his own understanding he has realized the heart's release, the release by insight, and having attained it dwells therein."

Still, few monks succeed in this endeavour according to SN LV, XI, VI, iii (V, 406).

Those who do not understand the four noble Truths including knowing the practice of the Path that leads to the ending of suffering, will not reach release. But those who understand these Truths will be "blessed with the heart's release, blessed with release by insight," (the latter is *paññāvimuttiyā*).

Besides, all *Arahant*s have full understanding of the four noble Truths, as they really are. And finally, in him who knows, who sees the four noble Truths there is destruction of the *āsava*s. Not in him who knows not, who sees not. These ideas can be found in three successive *sutta*s in the SN, namely SN LVI, XII, III, ii-iv (V, 432-4). Together these teachings offer a picture of the connections between the Truths, the *āsava*s and release.

— In conclusion on the search of the *Saṁyutta Nikāya* by means of the index to the PTS edition, those who understand the four noble Truths will be blessed with the heart's release, blessed with release by insight and so there is calm and insight (SN LVI, XII, III, ii-V, 432-3). However, calm and insight also have to be cultivated (*bhāvetabbā*) by full comprehension (SN XLV, I, I, xi -V, 52), and are reached by the eightfold Path and not by a more specific method (SN 35.204-IV, 195).

The destruction of the *āsavas* may be another result of understanding the four noble Truths (SN LVI, XII, III, v-V, 434). However, apparently there are also other interpretations on the function of the taints: destruction of the *āsavas* can win release of heart, release by insight (SN LV, XI, III, iv-V, 376). So the destruction of the taints may be consequence or cause of release.

A third variant in SN XLVIII, IV, V, v ff.-(V, 222 f.) teaches that after the destruction of the *āsavas*, still the controlling faculties, especially *paññā*, have to be developed to reach the wisdom that is awakening.

4.2.3 Check by means of the internet

To check whether we missed *sutta*s with important information on how to develop *vipassanā*, we searched with the term 'vipassana'on the internet-site www.accesstoinsight.org, which in this site means a subject, not an index term. We traced fewer references than already discussed above in this way, and there was a lot of overlap with the results already found.

The most interesting reference is to *sutta* MN 7 (I, 36), which we will discuss below. Furthermore, this site offers one reference to the *Khuddaka-Nikāya*: namely *Dhammapada* verse 372, which we quoted already in par. 2.2.3, to show the importance of developing the balance and harmony between *jhāna* and wisdom. Still, this trail was useful as it led to Dhp 373 and 374, translated by Buddharakhita. We summarize these as follows. After calming the mind, a monk who has comprehended the Dhamma with insight has reached (*vipassato*) a more than human delight (Dhp 373). According to Dhp 374, when one sees with right insight (*sammā-sati*) the rise and fall of the elements of existence, one is full of joy. This reflects the deathless to the discerning one.

Furthermore, Thanissaro Bhikkhu (www.accesstoinsight.org, 04.07. 2010) translated *paññāvimutto* with "released through discernment" in AN 9.44 (IV, 452). Consequently, we do not have to use the same translation 'insight' for *paññā* as for *vipassanā,* nor the rather vague 'wisdom'. Instead one may use discernment for *paññā*.

Besides *sutta* AN 10.60 (V, 108) advises to reflect on ten perceptions: perceptions of inconstancy, of not-self, of unattractiveness of the body, of pains and drawbacks of the body, of abandoning of thoughts of sensuality, of cessation of fabrications, of the ending of craving etc.[74] Then that *sutta* continues with training in *sati*. In this part on *sati* of AN 10.60 (V, 108) the search term 'vipassana' is added in brackets by the translator, Piyadassi Thera.

According to MN 7, the *Vatthūpama-sutta,* a monk first gets rid of the defilements of the mind. Knowing these as defilements leading to a bad destination, he gets rid of them. This is compared to a cloth that has to be cleaned before dyeing it. Then he develops faith in the triple gem and by means of joy, calm and happiness reaches a concentrated mind. Following the exercises in MN 7, next the monk dwells in the four *brahma-vihara*s (meditation exercises), and then "He comprehends: 'There is this, there is a low, there is the excellent, there is a further escape from perceptions.'"

[74] Woodward (1936) 1955: 74 translates: "ideas", instead of "perceptions" in Piyadassi Thera's translation.

The meaning of this sentence is not explained in the *sutta.*[75] However, the result of comprehending is freedom:

> "For one thus knowing, thus seeing, the mind is freed from the canker of sense-pleasures and ... becoming ... and ignorance. In freedom the knowledge comes to him that he is freed," (MN 7-I, 38)

I.B. Horner (1954: 48 n. 7) notes that traditionally the practice of the *brahmavihāra*s allegedly leads to the company of Brahmā, but in this *sutta* MN 7 these meditations lead to *Nibbāna* according to the commentary. The *Tevijja-Sutta* (DN 13) forms an example of *brahmavihāra*s which may lead to Brahmā. Interestingly, these meditations in MN 7 lead to comprehension, knowledge and freedom from the taints. That makes it understandable to regard the Pali MN 7 as a teaching on *vipassanā,* as the website "accesstoinsight" does. Besides, the *brahmavihāras* are meditation exercises.

— Searching the internet-site www.accesstoinsight.org with the term 'vipassana' leads to the following conclusions.

Though the characteristics of existence are not found in the *Vatthūpama-Sutta* (MN 7), this *sutta* still leads to freedom from ignorance, but by means of a for Pali *sutta*s rather untraditional way. So comparison with the Chinese rendering would be useful.

According to AN 10.60 (V, 108) one contemplates first the perceptions of the characteristics of existence, and then mindfulness (*sati*) has to be trained. We note that this order seems unusual. Insight in the *Dhamma* or the rise and fall of the elements of existence (*khandha*s) leads to delight or joy (Dhp 373 and 374).

In Dhp 374 *sammā-sati* has been translated with 'insight', instead of by right mindfulness. *Sutta* SN XLVII, III, I, vi (V, 148) only concerns *sati*, but 'vipassana' is added in the translator's comments, without explaining the connection. So, some translators seem to see *sati* as a synonym of *vipassanā.*

Translation of *paññāvimutto* with "released through discernment" avoids using 'insight' for *paññā*, and that prevents confusion with *vipassanā*.

[75] A possible explanation of this sentence may be found in notes to the PTS translation (1954: 48). According to note 4, "this" refers in the commentary on MN (I, 176) to "the attainment of arahantship".

4.3 Conclusion on the development of *vipassanā* in Pali canonical sources

In this conclusion we discuss which principles related to insight and its development, are widely accepted in the Pali *suttas*. Finally, we suggest which Pali *suttas* offer more or less complete methods to reach enlightenment including these principles, and which *suttas* can add the aspects we miss.

The characteristics of existence, which are impermanence, suffering, and this is not my self (*anicca, dukkha, anattā*), must be seen with insight according to *suttas* such as MN 22 (I, 138 f.) and MN 74. *Sutta* AN 7.46 (IV, 46) explains that the perception of impermanence offers a basis to develop first insight into suffering, and then perception of not my self may be developed.

According to the method of MN 74 (I, 499 f.), such insight in those characteristics of existence is based on the body consisting of four elements and the impermanence of feelings. Seeing feelings in this way one gets enough of feelings, one becomes passionless and is freed. Sāriputta, hearing this, contemplated it and was freed from the taints according to MN 74 (I, 501).

The Theravāda version of MN 148 is dealing purely with insight, since it teaches impermanence, not the self, abandoning the tendencies to feelings to arouse true knowledge. Seeing thus can lead towards the end of suffering by not clinging and to liberation from the taints.

The destruction of the taints of lust, becoming and ignorance (the *āsavas*) is mentioned in many *suttas* in relation to insight, knowledge, seeing or wisdom. For example, by the destruction of the taints, freedom through wisdom can be reached according to MN 6 (I, 35-6), AN 3.89 (I, 235) and AN 4.5 (II, 6). So the discourses mentioned in the two sections above corroborate those who teach that the characteristics (or marks) of existence and the destruction of the taints are typical of *vipassana*.

In many of the *suttas* discussed belonging to the DN (such as DN 22-II, 313 ff.), the four *jhānas* are part of the process to develop a profound knowledge (*aññā*), which means becoming an Arahant. In DN 29 (III, 132) the *jhānas* are combined with the destruction of the taints and with deliverance by wisdom.

There are also some *suttas* in the MN (MN 141-III, 252; MN 117-III, 75 f.) and in the SN (SN XXXV, IV, 5, 204 (IV, 195) which teach that the four *jhānas* are a necessary part of the way leading to the cessation of suffering. In MN 141 wisdom or insight is not mentioned, an explanation might be that the disciple Sāriputta trains the monks here for the fruit of stream-entry.

However, several MN and AN *suttas* teach that in the first *jhāna* or a higher concentration, liberation by insight may be reached by contemplation of *jhāna* (MN 52-I, 350; MN 64-I, 435; AN 9.36-IV, 422 ff. and AN 11.17-V, 343).

So, insight through *jhāna* and insight in the characteristics of existence are each mentioned several times as liberating. Release by insight which is freed from the *āsavas* is another common formula. Section 4.2.1.1 above mentions more references to relevant discourses.

The methods vary as well: from development of mindfulness (*sati*, in particular of breathing or of the body), following the eightfold Path, to contemplation that the five constituents of 'a person' consist of the four (or up to six) elements.

4.3.1 Summary of methods leading to insight

One may want to avoid taking parts from many *suttas* to describe a method leading to insight. Combining many discourses would complicate understanding or instruction more than necessary, and many *suttas* also contain elements less related to insight. Only few *suttas* combine most of the elements related to insight, namely the characteristics of existence, and the destruction of the taints together with a sufficient level of concentration in a single teaching. Consequently, these may be most suitable for training purposes towards liberating insight.

Sutta DN 2 (I, 60 ff.) goes a long way to teach how to develop all aspects of concentration and insight. The final insight reached is in the origin and destruction of the taints. A teaching which specifically develops insight in impermanence (*anicca*), such as found in MN 118 (III, 83 f.); MN 146 (III, 270 ff.) or AN 7.46 (IV, 46 ff.), might be added to complete the method.

Sutta DN 22 (II, 290 ff.) offers another almost complete method to develop insight, with more extensive training in mindfulness. Here *anattā* is implicit in origination - dissolution of the body, because of our lack of control over it, it is impermanent and not as we wish. Therefore it is non-self. A combination of DN 22 with MN 62 adds an explicit method to understand *anattā*, completing the three insights in the characteristics of existence. The last exercises of DN 22 (II, 304 ff.) concern contemplation of the four noble Truths, which include full insight in suffering and its cause. *Sutta* DN 22 leads to either becoming an *Arahant* or a non-returner. However, the taints of craving for becoming and ignorance have not been mentioned in DN 22. *Sutta* SN 47.50 (V, 189 f.) connects DN 22 with the destruction of the taints thus: "For eliminating these three taints, O monks, the four Foundations of Mindfulness should be cultivated."

The discourses MN 64 (I, 435 ff.) and AN 9.36 (IV, 422 ff.) have a different approach from the above *sutta*s: these teach contemplation during *jhāna* to see *anicca, dukkha*, and *anattā.* Then one has to concentrate on the sublime (*nibbāna*), which according to MN 64 (I, 436 f.) finally may destroy the taints.

Sutta MN 118 teaches to observe the process of breathing. One trains to develop penetrative awareness of the impermanent nature of reality and to observe detachment, stopping and casting away of craving and grief for the world (MN 118-III, 83 f.). A similar method of concentration with mindfulness on in-breathing and out-breathing is also taught in the *Vinaya* (Vol. 1, III, 1, 3-III, 70-1). These may be regarded as practices specifically aimed at insight.[76]

Sutta MN 118 continues with realisation of the four foundations of mindfulness, and then the seven factors for awakening arise one by one, which include tranquillity. When the body is tranquil, thought is concentrated and the monk develops concentration. Looking with proper care at this, he develops equanimity. Though the level of concentration is not specified in MN 118, full development of the seven links of awakening is deemed to be sufficient for liberation in the text. However, MN 118 does not explicitly teach how to develop insight in *dukkha* and *anattā.*

We may consider MN 22 as complementary to MN 118 in these respects. According to MN 22 (I, 137 f.), seeing impermanence should lead on to insight into unsatisfactoriness and not my self, as it is not appropriate to see 'what is impermanent, unsatisfactory and subject to change as "this is my self". This process conduces one to turn away from the five elements of existence (*khandha*s). Thereby one is freed from passion, by being free from passion one is liberated and the knowledge that one is freed arises (MN 22-I, 139). This constitutes a method to become passionless without *jhāna* and leading to liberating insight. The *Vinaya* (*Mahāvagga* I, 6.38-

---

[76] Breet and Janssen 2005, MN vol. 3: 172 n. 113

41-I, 13-14) offers an alternative argument: one cannot control the elements of existence and so they are not self.

At least three discourses in the MN explain ways to develop insight and liberation without the four *jhāna*s: besides MN 22, we mention MN 74 and MN 148.

According to the method of MN 74 (I, 499 f.), insight in the three characteristics of existence is based on the body consisting of four elements and the impermanence of feelings. Seeing feelings in this way one gets enough of feelings, one becomes passionless, is freed and one knows this. Sāriputta, hearing this, contemplated it and was freed from the taints according to MN 74 (I, 501).

MN 148 is also dealing purely with insight, since it teaches impermanence, not the self, and abandoning the tendencies to feelings to arouse true knowledge. Seeing thus can lead towards the end of suffering by disenchantment with feeling and with craving, leading to dispassion. Hearing this led some monks to not clinging and to liberation from the taints.

Sutta MN 4 explains the four *jhāna*s, leading to understanding of the four Truths and the taints. *Sutta* AN 3.88 (I, 235) calls the understanding of the four Truths the training in the higher insight, and this may be combined with AN 3.89 (I, 235 f.) which states that the training in the higher insight destroys the taints. These *sutta*s support the teaching in MN 4 (I, 23) that such understanding of the four noble Truths and of the taints lead to knowledge of release by insight.

Table 2. This table summarizes some *sutta*s leading to insight.
'Marks' = characteristics of existence.

Sutta(s)	Concept	Method	Which Insight?
DN 2	How to develop the fruits.	*Sīla, sati*, develop insights; focus on taints.	Origin and destruction of taints.
DN 22; MN 62	Mindfulness	*Sati* exercises; origination - dissolution of 4 elements.	The four noble Truths.
MN 64; AN 9.36	Destruction of the taints.	First *jhāna* or a higher concentration; contemplate *jhāna*.	Focus on the deathless element: peace …destruction of craving, the cool.
MN 118 and MN 22	Awareness of impermanence.	Observe the process of breathing.	Knowledge that one is freed.
MN 74 (I, 500-1); MN 148	Seeing the three marks of existence.	Consider the marks of body and feelings and get enough of these.	Into impermanence, unsatisfactoriness and this is not my self. Abandoning leaning to feelings ends dukkha.
MN 4, AN 3.88 (I, 235) and AN 3.89 (I, 235f.)	Four *jhāna*s. Three trainings.	Training in higher virtue, higher mind and higher wisdom.	Understanding the four noble Truths and the taints. Knowledge of release.

Concentration	See any characteristics?	Final step
Four *jhāna*s.	*Anattā, dukkha.*	Destruction of taints of lust, becoming, ignorance.
Four *jhāna*s.	*Anicca, dukkha.* MN 62: *anattā.*	Contemplate the arising and vanishing of mental factors, or know these exist.
In a *jhāna.*	See in *jhāna*: *anicca, dukkha, anattā.*	Concentrating on the sublime, (*nibbāna*) destroys the taints.
Calm the body, then a concentrated mind arises (MN 118).	*Anicca, dukkha, anattā.*	Freedom from passion.
	Anicca, dukkha, anattā.	Freedom of desire/passion.
		MN 148: by dispassion to liberation.
Higher mind is four *jhāna*s, including pure *sati* by equanimity.		Lust, hatred and delusion are destroyed. Dispassion.

Chapter 5

The development of *vipassanā* in some *Āgama-sūtras* compared with the Pali

How does the development of insight in Pali canonical sources compare with related *Āgama-sūtras* in Chinese sources, as far as available in English? We look for texts of schools that were geographically distant from the Theravāda tradition to limit late cross influences. The purpose is to find which ideas found in the Pali texts are corroborated by another tradition. Alternatively, some ideas deemed important in the Pali texts might be less so according to Chinese renderings. To call this refutation would go too far, as our translated material is limited.

An example of the limitations of the translated material concerns DN 2. The section with the discourse of the Buddha describing the training of the *śramaṇa*, which we would have liked to compare with DN 2, has been left out from the translation in '*A study of the Śrāmaṇyaphala-sūtra*'.[77] However, its author G. Macqueen confirms that one of the Chinese manuscripts he used contains the complete training. He mentions the sequence from moral behaviour through meditational and psychic attainments to the destruction of the *asrāvas*, the knowledge of this destruction, and the victory over rebirth. According to Macqueen (1988: 181), 'For our present purposes the main point to be made is that the ancient text must have included this document.' Still, we cannot test the specific ideas related to insight.

---

[77] G. Macqueen 1988: 46, 178-180). In the discussion on DN 2 we remarked that this complete practice was taught to king Ajātasattu, who had killed his father and only confesses this and becomes a lay follower of the Buddha at the very end of that *sutta*. According to Macqueen (1988: 184) 'Ajatasatru confesses his crime of patricide and begs the Buddha to accept his confession. The Buddha does so (P, CI, C2, Tb, S).' So the criminal record and late confession are common to the Pali, two Chinese, the Tibetan and the Sanskrit redactions.

5.1 Mindfulness to develop insight in Chinese and Pali discourses

The *Smṛtyupasthānasūtra* of the *Ekottara-Āgama* (EA) is translated from the Chinese version as the 'Discourse on the cultivation of recollection' (Bhikkhu Pāsādika, 1998). Since the monk cultivates *sati* and concentration, we will compare this *sūtra* with DN 22. At the beginning the Chinese text mentions the parts of the eightfold Way. Then several exercises are taught, in which impure substances of the body, the four material elements of the body as well as a dead body in all phases are contemplated. This leads to: "this body of his is impermanent and subject to breaking up." (Transl. Pāsādika, 1998: 498)

This is more explicit than DN 22 where the repeated awareness of rising and vanishing may lead to insight in impermanence, though the term is not mentioned there. The Chinese refrain is brief: "In this way a *bhikṣu* contemplates his body and feels happy [after having] overcome evil thoughts and become free from sadness and lamentation." (Transl. Pāsādika, 1998: 496-498) The contemplation of breathing and some of the other body meditations that are known in the DN version, are absent from the EA redaction.

The *Dīgha-Nikāya* version of the *sutta* explains the four noble Truths extensively, leading to a deep knowledge of suffering. The EA rendering only offers specific aspects of this system. The latter version describes contemplation of feelings and of the mind; thereafter the Chinese rendering continues with the cultivation of "right concentration" as follows. After the *bhikṣu* has cultivated right recollection and wakefulness together with diligence, he cultivates right concentration.

The description of the first stage reads:

> "By relying on contemplation rather than inclination and on cessation, [namely] (viz.) the abolition of all that is karmically unwholesome, the *bhikṣu* thus contemplates *dharma*s and settles his mind. Then the *bhikṣu*, free from desire and having overcome all that is karmically unwholesome, [experiences] the first absorption in which there is thinking, deliberation and one's mindfully experiencing happiness."
>
> (Transl. Pāsādika, 1998: 501)

After that follows a description of the way to reach each of the four absorptions. Thereafter it is stated: "In this way the *bhikṣu* contemplates *dharmas* and settles his mind." He contemplates what is subject to origination and dissolution. This section on cultivation of concentration in the EA is similar to DN 22 in the fourth pillar of mindfulness.

In the DN version, the final exercise is again the refrain including: "He abides contemplating arising phenomena in mind-objects, he abides contemplating vanishing phenomena in mind-objects" (DN 22-II, 314, Walshe 1987: 349). According to the EA redaction, in this way "beings can achieve purification, abolish sadness and lamentation, transcend the notions of lamentation and joy, win insight-knowledge and realise Nirvāṇa" (transl. Pāsādika, 1998: 501). DN 22 does conclude that the fruit is a profound knowledge (*aññā*), and that means becoming an Arahant or a non-returner.[78]

> — So these discourses on mindfulness DN 22 and the *Ekottara-Āgama* 'Discourse on the cultivation of recollection' do not mention insight in 'non-self', the destruction of the taints, and the concept *vipassanā-bhāvanā* (the development of insight). Still sufficient knowledge is reached to realise *Nirvāṇa* or at least non-return. This profound knowledge (*aññā*) in DN 22 and insight-knowledge in the translation from the EA have not been specified.
>
> Bhikkhu Sujato (2010, Ch. 3) has stated that DN 22 is nothing more than a late expansion of MN 10 and the four noble Truths were taken from MN 141. He did not offer an argument for this point. However, we saw that the Chinese *Smṛtyupasthānasūtra* of the EA refers to the fourth noble Truth, by mentioning the parts of the eightfold Way and including methods to reach the four absorptions as well. So this partly supports the DN rendering.
>
> According to the classification of Anālayo (2008: 12-4), we would classify the EA rendering as 'related' to DN 22, as these discourses do show some very specific and characteristic similarities to each other, but have important differences as well.

The 'Discourse on the Foundations of Mindfulness' of the *Madhyama-Āgama* (MA) contains several contemplations on the body as the body such as on its positions, on breathing, on the impure substances of the body, and on human remains. However, one of the other contemplations of the body seems to refer to a concentration method. We quote: "Again,

[78] T.W. and C.A.F. Rhys Davids mention in DN 22 that *aññā* is an epithet of *arahant*ship (PTS 1910: 346); Walshe (1987: 350) translates *aññā* directly with 'Arahantship'.

oh *Bhikṣus*, in contemplating the body as the body, a *Bhikṣu* fills his body throughout with rapture and bliss born out of concentration, saturating and moistening it." (Transl. Saddhaloka, 1983: 11)

Each contemplation results in mindfulness and insight, as stated in the following part of the refrain: "Establishing mindfulness in the body, there is knowledge, there is insight, there is understanding, and there is penetration." (Transl. Saddhaloka, 1983: 9 ff.) The same results are obtained by contemplating the feelings as the feelings and the mind as the mind, the six internal sense-bases and the five hindrances.

Then "mindfulness" has been mentioned as the first of the seven factors of enlightenment as well, which are part of *dharma*s.[79] The meditating *bhikṣu* should know its presence, or absence, or its arising and development. However, for each factor of enlightenment except the first (mindfulness) and the last (equanimity), this Chinese text abridges thereby avoiding repetitions according to the translator Saddhaloka (1983, 15, n. 19). This poses the problem that there is no specific description at all for 'concentration' among the factors of enlightenment. Apparently, in this structure it seems implied that the monk should just be fully aware of his state of concentration.

The result is once more: "Establishing mindfulness in the dharmas, there is knowledge, there is insight, there is understanding, and there is penetration." (Saddhaloka, 1983: 15)

When someone is dwelling in these four foundations of mindfulness, then "either he attains to the supreme knowledge as a manifest dharma, or if there is a residue he or she attains to Non-returner." (Saddhaloka, 1983: 15)

— We propose the following conclusions on the *Madhyama-Āgama* redaction of the 'Discourse on the Foundations of Mindfulness'. Concentration is probably an object of contemplation in this MA text, both in a body-contemplation and as a factor of enlightenment. Therefore concentration is mainly a means to develop mindfulness.

In the MA rendering of this discourse on mindfulness, established mindfulness leads to insight and deep understanding of body and mind, sufficient for liberation by insight or attainment of the state of non-returner. These points also apply to MN 10. However,

[79] In this context *Dharma*s mean mental contents, mental objects (Saddhaloka 1983: 15, n. 16).

the contents of that insight are not made explicit in the MA version, while in MN 10 he understands the four noble Truths.

Consequently, we would call these *sutta*s 'partial parallels' in Anālayo's classification as many characteristic teachings agree, but the insight does not.

The *Saṁyukta-Āgama* (SA) also contains a *sūtra* on mindfulness of breathing (SA 810) which we will compare with MN 118.[80]

The core subject of the *Ānāpānasati-Sutta* (MN 118) and SA 810 (T II 208a-c) is the same: observe the process of breathing, to be trained in sixteen phases. During the last group of four exercises, one trains to develop penetrative awareness of the impermanent nature of reality and to contemplate detachment, stopping and casting away (MN 118-III, 83). The order and terminology in the Chinese *sūtra* of this last group are somewhat different. After contemplating impermanence follow contemplation of eradication, dispassion, and cessation in SA 810.
However, in Anālayo's translation (2007: 149) of the phases of SN 54.13 (SN V, 328-33), impermanence, dispassion and cessation figure as well, but the order still differs from the Chinese rendering and the SN has relinquishment instead of eradication. The last four exercises may be regarded as practices specifically aimed at insight.

After realizing the four foundations of mindfulness the seven factors of awakening arise one by one, which include tranquillity. When the body is tranquil, thought is concentrated and the monk develops concentration. Looking with proper care at this, he develops equanimity. This sequence is similar in MN 118 and SA 810. Though the level of concentration is not specified in these *sutta*s, full development of the seven links of awakening seems to be sufficient for liberation. Anālayo (2007: 148-9) concludes on his comparison of SA 810 and SN 54.13:

> 'Looking back on the two versions as a whole, however, the instructions on how to develop mindfulness of breathing in sixteen phases agree closely. This sixteen fold scheme, described in both versions, shows how a particular instance of contemplation of the body – mindfulness of breathing – can be developed in such a way as to cover all

---

[80] Anālayo translated SA 810 and compared this *sutta* with SN 54.13 in BSR 24.2, 2007. Comparison with MN 118 seems a useful addition, even more so as SN 54.13 has been abbreviated in the PTS translation.

four *satipaṭṭhāna*s and lead to the development of seven factors of awakening and thereby to liberation.'

— We suggest that this conclusion is applicable as well to the comparison of SA 810 and MN 118. Anālayo interprets 'liberation' as the final goal of all mindfulness practices thus: "mental purification and attainment of Nibbāna." Yet, neither MN 118 nor SA 810 explicitly teaches how to develop two important aspects of *vipassanā,* namely insight in *dukkha* and *anattā*. The taints are not mentioned either.

Using Anālayo's (2008: 12-14) classification, we suggest that these *sutta*s MN 118, SA 810 and SN 54.13 are parallels as the main teachings agree, although the order of some points disagrees. The *Ānāpāna* version in the EA is different from these texts and may, according to Thich Huyèn-Vi (BSR 1993, 2: 213), be compared with MN 62.

5.2 Insight in the *Madhyama-Āgama* and the *Majjhima-Nikāya*

Regrettably, we did not trace translations from the Chinese renderings of those *Majjhima-Nikāya sutta*s which were considered in paragraph 4.3 to teach more or less complete methods to reach enlightenment (an exception is the partial parallel to MN 10). Therefore, we will test the results of the above analysis of Pali texts by comparison of principles often connected with the development of insight. This analysis will be mainly based on the comparative study by Thich Minh Chau (ca. 1964) of the *Madhyama-Āgama* and the MN. This scholar asserts that the MA represents the tenets of the Sarvāstivāda School (Thich Minh Chau ca. 1964: 18).

5.2.1 The concepts of insight, knowledge, seeing, and wisdom

We begin with a comparative analysis of the concepts of insight, knowledge, seeing, or wisdom. Do these concepts related to insight receive a similar treatment in the *Majjhima-Nikāya* and the *Madhyama-Āgama*?

There exists an MA discourse related to MN 148, the latter being one of the Pali discourses most dedicated to insight. However, according to Sujato the Pali shows many differences with the Sarvāstivāda version in

MA 86. 'Both the setting and the contents of the Sarvāstivāda version display considerable divergence, especially the inclusion of many groups of dhammas dealing with meditation and samādhi practice, thus altering the pure insight orientation of the Theravāda version.' (Sujato 2012: 318). Lacking an English translation, we must conclude that the Chinese rendering does not offer support for the insight without concentration method.

The Chinese MA *sūtra* No. 93 (Tse vi, 12b-13b) agrees with MN 7, the *Vatthūpama-sutta,* that by knowing the defilements a monk gets rid of these. However, the MA version has 21 defilements and the MN rendering lists 16 (Thich Minh Chau (ca.) 1964: 230). The teaching on the *brahmavihāras* or immeasurables is almost the same as well (Thich Minh Chau (ca.) 1964: 231). According to the Pali MN 7 (I, 38), the successful training in the immeasurables leads to understanding of the existence of an escape from this world, destruction of the taints and the knowledge of being liberated. However, the Chinese rendering does not offer the resulting understanding, destruction of the taints, and freedom by these contemplations or meditations, but only agrees with the Pali that this is washing clean the inner mind (Thich Minh Chau (ca.) 1964: 231).

— A liberating knowledge is lacking in this Chinese rendering MA 93. So this text does not corroborate our conclusion in par. 4.2.3 on the Pali MN 7 that it can be considered as a text on *vipassanā-bhāvanā* or the development of insight. Besides, the Chinese version has not mentioned destruction of the taints. So in this case also we would call these discourses 'partial parallels' (Anālayo's 2008: 12-14 terminology), as many characteristic teachings agree but the fruit (result) does not.

According to the Pali redaction of MN 56 (I, 380), the hearing of the four noble Truths leads to stream-winning of a citizen. Then 'the Dhamma eye which was free from dust arose in him: "Whatever was liable to be born was also liable to cease"' (Thich Minh Chau (ca. 1964: 285-6). This citizen overcame uncertainty as well. However, according to Thich Minh Chau (ca. 1964: 286), the parallel sentence in the Chinese version MA 133 (Tse vi, 55b-59a) states that Yu-p'o-li, perceived the four noble Truths and thereby overcame uncertainty about the *Dhamma.*

— Therefore, the Chinese redaction of MA 133 does not support the insight "Whatever was liable to be born was also liable to cease" of MN 56. Still, both versions refer to an important aspect of stream-entry: overcoming uncertainty about the *Dhamma*.

According to the Chinese discourse MA 14 (Tse vi, 16b-17b), the monk addressed should reflect whether the deed brings suffering. However, even if a 'bodily deed was not permissible, but for oneself and for others it would bring meritorious fruit and happiness, than he should perform such a bodily deed.' (Thich Minh Chau ca. 1964: 131 f., 292 f.)

Sutta MN 61 instructs Rāhula to consider at each bodily, verbal and mental action whether it leads to more suffering for oneself or others. If so one should abstain, if possible. Both renderings train to consider whether one causes suffering and so offer insight in that mark of existence, but the Chinese allows a wider interpretation of what is acceptable. The results in the Chinese version are that one becomes prosperous, happy, secure and fearless (Thich Minh Chau ca. 1964:184). The result according to the Pali text is purification of all actions.

— Consequently, these discourses MA 14 and MN 61 offer insight in the characteristic of existence of suffering. However, they do not lead to liberating insight. Besides the results that can be reached differ in the two versions. Using Anālayo's (2008: 12-14) terminology, we would call these *sutta*s partial parallels, as many characteristic teachings agree but the fruits (results) do not.

In the Chinese rendering MA 211, right view associates with five factors "to obtain fruit of freedom of mind, fruit of freedom of wisdom", and to obtain the merits of these (Thich Minh Chau ca. 1964: 261). These factors are to associate with truth, with moral conduct, with extensive hearing, with quietude and finally "to associate with insight." (MA 211-Tse vii, 85a-87a)

Sāriputta teaches in MN 43 (I, 293) that "intuitive wisdom" is to be developed thus:

"*Idh' āvuso sammādiṭṭhi sīlānuggahītā ca hoti sutānuggahītā ca hoti sākacchānuggahītā ca hoti samathānuggahītā ca hoti vipassanānuggahītā ca hoti.*" (MN 43-I, 294)

According to the PTS translation of this *sutta,* moral habit, hearing, discussion, calm and vision forward right understanding. We note that in this case *vipassanā* has been rendered with 'vision', while in this research we often translated it with "insight". In MN 43 *vipassanā* is part of a process to develop right understanding, not a result. The results mentioned in this *sutta* are freedom of mind, "and the fruit of freedom through intuitive wisdom and the advantage of the fruit of freedom through intuitive wisdom." (MN 43-I, 294)

— We observe that "insight" is a factor to acquire "wisdom" in both the Chinese MA 211 and Pali MN 43. Thich Minh Chau (ca. 1964: 145) suggests that these texts show how to obtain mind-freedom and wisdom-freedom. We conclude that *vipassanā* is part of a process to develop freedom through wisdom (MA) or freedom through intuitive wisdom (MN). We traced no support in the sources about the MA for a method that solely develops insight towards liberation, such as we found in the Pali discourses MN 74 and MN 148.

5.2.2 Insight and the taints

How are insight, knowledge, seeing, or wisdom related to the destruction of the taints (*āsava*s-cankers, influxes) according to the MA?

According to Thich Minh Chau's rendering (ca. 1964: 216), a Chinese text in MA 10 (Tse, v, 13a-b) states: "It is through knowledge, through vision that cankers are extinguished, not without knowledge, without vision." The following cankers (taints) are mentioned in this section of the MA version:

> "With right consideration, the not yet arisen cankers of sense-desire do not arise; the already arisen cankers then disappear; the not yet arisen cankers of becoming, cankers of ignorance do not arise; the already arisen cankers then disappear." (Thich Minh Chau ca. 1964: 216)

These taints correspond with the PTS English and Pali renderings of *sutta* MN 2 (I, 7), namely: sense-pleasure (*kāmāsavo*), becoming (*bhavāsavo*), and ignorance (*avijjāsavo*). Bhikkhu Anālayo (2011, lecture 6) translates these taints with sensual desire, existence and ignorance. There are seven methods to get rid of taints in both versions of this *sutta.* According to Anālayo (2011, lecture 6), these methods treat the same subjects in Pali and Chinese but have been presented in a different order.

External irritants such as mosquitoes and dangers have been called 'cankers' as well in these two *sutta*s, but these are not relevant here. Anālayo notes the main points to practice for overcoming the *āsava*s in his lecture. However, the results of eliminating all taints by applying these methods are different. According to the Pali MN 2 the monk has destroyed craving, removed the fetters, understood conceit and he has ended suffering. When all taints have been abandoned, Ñāṇamoli and Bodhi (1995: 96) translate the result of MN 2 thus:

> "He has severed craving, flung off the fetters, and with the complete penetration of conceit he has made an end to suffering."

On the other hand, the Chinese rendering states that when "this monk has eradicated all cankers, [he] is emancipated from fetters, [he] is able to use right wisdom to put an end to suffering." (Thich Minh Chau ca. 1964: 222)

— While in the Pali MN 2 the elimination of the taints sense/sensual-desire, becoming and ignorance means liberation, the Chinese MA 10 offers a possibility of liberation. Consequently, we would call these *sutta*s 'partial parallels' as many characteristic teachings on how to destroy the taints agree, but the fruits are different, at least according to the translations. The order of some points also differs.

MA sutta No. 81 (Tse, v, 114b) teaches attention to the body. When attention to the body is fully developed one has access to the psychic powers culminating in "the knowledge of life and death. Then with the eradication of the cankers, he knows and realizes by himself here-now and dwells in mind-emancipation, wisdom-emancipation, which is cankerless, he attains arahantship." The final part of MN 119 does not make the attainment of *Arahant*-ship explicit, but otherwise contains the same subjects leading to destruction of the taints, and liberation of mind and by wisdom. Apparently this also means *Arahant*-ship. According to Thich Minh Chau (ca. 1964: 145), several other MN and MA *sutta*s mention freedom of mind and freedom by wisdom as well. However, he does not show these comparative studies in that book.

— In the case of MA 81 and MN 119, when attention to the body has been fully developed, finally wisdom (MA) or intuitive wisdom (MN) goes together with destruction of the taints and liberation.

5.2.3 The taints and liberation

Does the MA corroborate the idea in the Pali *sutta*s that destruction of the taints (or cankers) means liberation? Which taints do these texts distinguish? How does the treatment of the taints correspond or differ? Does insight in the three characteristics of existence (impermanence, suffering and not mine) play an important role in the MA?

Freedom of mind, and freedom through wisdom may be attained here and now by the strong wish to destroy the taints, according to both MN 6 (I, 35-6) and MA 105 (Tse, vi, 29a-29b).[81]

According to MA No. 102 (Tse, vi, 24 b, 6-9) once he has reached a purified and concentrated mind, "well fixed and immovable, he bends his mind towards the extinction of the cankers, towards knowledge of attainment, towards realization." (Thich Minh Chau ca. 1964: 148) Then he knows the four noble Truths as they really are. "He also knows these cankers as they really are".

Such knowledge and vision imply that the mind is freed from the taints of sense-desire, becoming and ignorance. Knowing this he is emancipated (an *Arahant*), birth is destroyed. There is a corresponding text in Pali MN 19 which "is almost the same" according to Thich Minh Chau (ca. 1964: 149).

— Indeed, we see no difference in the teaching between this section of MN 19 (I, 117 par. 22-3) and the part of MA 102 just discussed, although the Pali concerns the awakening of the Buddha. The final knowledges concern the four noble Truths and the taints and this leads to liberation.

Sutta MA 204 (Tse, vii, 73b-76b) contains teachings related to MN 26. According to the Chinese MA 204, if someone abides in the fourth *dhyāna*, that state leads to obtaining the unshakable mind. The next step is thus: "He engages in mental training, cankers vanish, knowledge dawns, realization matures." (Thich Minh Chau ca. 1964: 250) Then he knows the four noble truths and the taints. His mind is free from the three taints.

According to MN 26 (the *Ariyapariyesana-Sutta*) a monk has to develop the four *jhānas*, followed by the *arūpajhānas* and cessation of perceptions and feelings. Finally, because he has seen with intuitive wisdom,

[81] Thich Minh Chau (ca.) 1964: 226.

the monk reaches the destruction of the taints ("*paññāya c'assa disvā āsavā parikkhīṇā honti*."). Then he is no longer attached to the world.

— So both MA 204 and MN 26 teach the four *jhāna*s as steps towards the destruction of the taints (cankers). However, the further 'mental training' to destroy the taints is unspecified in MA 204, but it comprises the *arūpajhāna*s and intuitive wisdom in MN 26 (I, 174-5). Though these texts are only partial parallels, the destruction of the cankers requiring concentration is the same.

An alternative way to become an Arahant is discussed in the Chinese MA 75 (Tse v, 103a-b), where all perceptions are to be considered as impermanent, suffering and subject to destruction. Then one has to see after reflection that no perception pertains to oneself, the mind is emancipated from the usual taints of sense-desire, becoming and ignorance. "Being emancipated, he knows that he is emancipated" (Thich Minh Chau ca. 1964: 149).

According to MN 106 (II, 265-6), the Pali *sutta* Thich Minh Chau compares with MA 75, considering everything as not mine leads to equanimity. When he does not grasp even that equanimity he reaches *nibbāna*, because he does not grasp anything. The taints are not mentioned in the Pali version. These two *sutta*s seem to stress the importance of developing the insight that nothing is mine.

— In MA 75 first the three characteristics of existence are developed with special attention to the insight that nothing is mine, and that means that the taints are destroyed and knowledge of emancipation is reached.

It is remarkable that "this is not the self" or "not mine" seems to be rare in the MA. Thich Minh Chau ca. 1964: 359) even does not mention *(an)-ātman*, *nairātmya* or *ātmagraha* in his list of Pali-Chinese-English equivalents. Neither has he mentioned (not) self in the "Index of some doctrinal terms" (Thich Minh Chau ca. 1964: 381-3).

Of course, not finding a concept does not prove it was not used. However, it seems worthwhile to try to refute the following working hypothesis: the concept "this is not the [my] self" or "not mine" is not important in the MA and the EA *sutta*s of which we have English translations.

5.3 Insight in the *Ekottara-Āgama* and the *Aṅguttara-Nikāya*

Besides the *Smṛtyupasthānasūtra* already discussed in section 5.1, we traced only a few translations from the Chinese *Ekottara-Āgama* which are relevant to our investigations on the development of insight.

A text in the *Ekottara-Āgama*, Eleventh Fascicle, Part 20, *sutta* 7 (further: EA 11.20.7) may be compared with *Sutta* AN 2.3.10 (I, 61).[82] We are going to quote the first half of the Chinese rendering and thereafter the core of the AN redaction.

> "Thus I have heard. At one time the Buddha was staying in Śrāvastī, ... the Exalted one said to the *bhikṣus*: A *bhikṣu* who lives in the forest (*āranyaka*) should cultivate two things. Which two? Tranquility (*śamatha*) and penetrating insight (*vipaśyana*). If a *bhikṣu*, living in the forest in serenity, realises tranquillity, he perfects the discipline (*vinaya*) with [all] its rules of moral training (*śikṣāpada*), without breaking the vows and by developing all virtues (*guṇa*). If, furthermore, a *bhikṣu* who is fond of solitude has realised penetrating insight, he exactly knows in accordance with fact: This is unsatisfactoriness (*duhkha*), the origin (*samudaya*) of unsatisfactoriness, its final cessation (*duhkhanirodha*) and what has necessarily to be done (*avaśyskārya*) in order to overcome unsatisfactoriness.
>
> By dint of such penetrating insight, his mind is freed from the malign influences of desire (*kāmāsrava*), of becoming (*bhavāsrava*) and of ignorance (*avidyāsrava*); consequently he gains the [insight-] knowledge of [this] freedom, knowing in accordance with fact: birth and death have come to an end, the holy life has been lived, what had to be done has been done, and there will be no more coming into existence." (EA 11.20.7)

In this EA version, tranquillity and *vipassanā* are connected with the four Truths, the freeing of the taints and knowledge of freedom. The second part of the EA *sutta* states that the Bodhisattva trained in the same way, "and furthermore, after realising penetrating insight, the Bodhisattva duly gained the state of possessing the three knowledges (*traividyatā*) and obtained the Highest, Complete and Full Enlightenment."

The redaction of AN 2.3.10 (I, 61) we can compare with EA 11.20.7 is translated by Sujato (2001: 27) as follows:

---

[82] Transl. of EA 11.20.7 by Thich Huyên-Vi and Bhikkhu Pāsādika, BSR 2001: 224-5.

"Monks, these two principles share in realization. What two? Samatha and vipassanā. When samatha is developed, what purpose is achieved? The mind is developed. When the mind is developed, what purpose is achieved? Lust is abandoned. When vipassanā is developed, what purpose is achieved? Understanding is developed. When understanding is developed, what purpose is achieved? Ignorance is abandoned. Monks, the mind tainted by lust is not released; understanding tainted by ignorance is not developed. Thus the release of heart is due to the fading away of lust; the release by understanding is due to the fading away of ignorance." (AN 2.3.10-I, 61)

— In conclusion, the Chinese EA *sutta* 11.20.7 gives a similar important role to the development of calm and insight as AN 2.3.10 (I, 61). In both texts calm and insight lead to liberation, but in this EA redaction desire is destroyed by means of insight, while the AN version attributes it to the development of the mind by means of *samatha*. Besides, the EA *sutta* refers to moral training and to virtues, which the Pali version does not.

The destruction of the three taints in the EA version, here translated as "malign influences", explicitly constitutes a last step to the knowledge that liberation is reached. These taints are the same as those which have been taught in many Pali *sutta*s but 'becoming' is absent from the AN redaction just discussed. The Chinese version corroborates the important role of the destruction of these taints as a last step to liberation taught in many Pali *sutta*s, as we already concluded on the MA.

So these *sutta*s are related, but the last step and the fruit are only partial parallels.

The *Ānāpāna [smṛti]-Sūtra* of the *Ekottara-Āgama*, seems to be related to MN 62 (Thich Huyên-Vi 1993: 213).[83] Already the first admonishing to Rāhula shows a difference between the Chinese and Pali versions. In the Chinese redaction Rāhula must contemplate form and the other constituents as impermanent, while in the Pali text he should see the five constituents by means of perfect intuitive wisdom thus: "this is not mine, this am I not, this is not my self" (MN 62-II, 421). Then according to the Chinese

[83] Transl. Thich Huyên-Vi and Bhikkhu Pāsādika, *Ekottara-Āgama*, sseventh fascicle, Part 17; *BSR* 1993, 2, 213 ff.

version, Rāhula concentrates and with one-pointedness of mind contemplates impermanence or, in the Pali text, focuses his attention to his direct surroundings. The Pali redaction gives much attention to meditation on the five elements, again to see this is "not-my- self" as it really is; while the Chinese omits this whole part. The advice to Rāhula to cultivate equanimity "so as to extirpate conceit (*māna*) and arrogance (*mada*)" is the only passage we may connect with the concept of "this is not my self" in the Chinese text.

Instruction to practice mindfulness of breathing figures in both discourses. According to the Pali Rāhula is pleased by these words. However, in the Chinese version Rāhula practices mindfulness of breathing and becomes fully aware. Then he wisely reflected on attachment and reached the four absorptions (*dhyānas*). He even remembered his former abodes and the birth and death of other beings. According to the EA *Ānāpāna-Sūtra*, he continues his efforts by what we would call the final stages of *vipassanā-bhāvanā* thus:

> "Moreover, he directed his mind to effect the destruction (*kṣaya*) of the mind's malign influences (*āsrava*). He realised and knew in accordance with fact: This is unsatisfactoriness (*duhkha*); he realised and knew in accordance with fact the origin (*samudaya*) of unsatisfactoriness, its final cessation (*duhkhanirodha*) and what has necessarily to be done (*avaśyskārya*) in order to overcome unsatisfactoriness."
>
> "By dint of such penetrating insight (*vipaśyana*) his mind was freed from the malign influences of desire (*kāmāsrava*) of becoming (*bhava*) and of ignorance (*avidyā*). Having realised [ultimate] freedom (*vimukti*), he gained the [insight-] knowledge of this freedom and knew in accordance with fact: Birth and death have come to an end, the holy life (*brahmacarya*) has been lived, what had to be done has been done, and there will be no more coming into existence."
>
> "At that time venerable Rāhula became an Arhat"
>
> (Thich Huyên-Vi 1993: 220)

— The EA *Ānāpāna-Sūtra* stresses the contemplation of impermanence, while the Pali MN 62 develops the insight that the constituents or the five elements of a 'person' are not the self. According to the EA text the four concentrations lead to knowledge of the four Truths, and penetrating insight frees him from the taints. Thereby he realises freedom and knows this. These partial parallel texts lead to very different results, as according to the Pali text Rāhula was pleased and in the Chinese rendering he became an *Arhat*.

5.4 Conclusions on some Chinese and Pali texts related to insight

We compared four Chinese MA redactions with presumably related Pali MN discourses to analyze their concepts of insight and wisdom. Of these four pairs only MA 211 and MN 43 agree that "insight" is a factor to acquire "wisdom". Apparently in this case *vipassanā* is part of a process to develop freedom through wisdom (MA) or freedom through intuitive wisdom (MN). The other three Chinese texts do not support a similar result.

Several Chinese discourses attach the same important role to the destruction of the same three taints as a last step to the knowledge that liberation has been reached as do many Pali *sutta*s. The Chinese *sūtra*s MA 81 and EA 11.20.7 corroborate Pali discourses such as MN 2, MN 7, and MN 119, stating that destruction of the taints and wisdom either go together with liberation or constitute a last step to the knowledge that liberation has been reached. When made explicit, the taints of desire, of becoming and of ignorance are the same as in many Pali *sutta*s. Furthermore, in both EA 11.20.7 and AN 2.3.10 (I, 61) calm and insight are needed for liberation.

According to MA 102 and MN 19 (I, 117 par. 22-3), the final kinds of knowledge concern the four noble Truths and the cankers (taints), and this leads to liberation. Both MA 204 and MN 26 (I, 174-5) teach the four *jhāna*s as steps towards the destruction of the taints (cankers). However, the further 'mental training' to destroy the taints is unspecified in MA 204, but the training comprises the *arūpa-jhāna*s and reaching intuitive wisdom in MN 26.

The discourses on the fourfold development of mindfulness we have discussed, namely the EA 'Discourse on the cultivation of recollection', DN 22, the MA 'Discourse on the Foundations of Mindfulness' and MN 10, do not mention insight in 'non-self'.

Furthermore, the destruction of the taints and the concept *vipassanā-bhāvanā* (the development of insight) are not found in these *sutta*s.

Still, sufficient knowledge is reached in all four discourses on the fourfold development of mindfulness to realise *Nirvāṇa* or at least non-return. The profound knowledge (*aññā*) in DN 22 and the supreme- respectively insight-knowledge in the translations from the MA and EA have not been specified. We suggest that the last point which one comes to know is at least part of this knowledge: in MA this is "equanimity" and in the other three discourses one finally understands the four noble Truths.

The Chinese and Pali discourses on mindfulness of breathing SA 810 and MN 118 show parallel patterns and results. According to MN 118, the seven factors of awakening bring to fulfilment freedom through knowledge. In SA 810 the final phase is: "having developed the equanimity factor of awakening in this way fulfils knowledge and liberation." While SN 54.13 concludes: "the seven limbs of wisdom complete knowledge and release." Yet, neither discourse explicitly teaches how to develop important aspects of *vipassanā,* namely insight in *dukkha* and *anattā* and destruction of the taints.

We traced the relationship of seeing all three characteristics of existence with the destruction of the cankers and knowledge of emancipation only in one MA sutta (MA 75-Tse, v, 103 a-b). However, impermanence is part of the Chinese discourses on mindfulness as discussed. Insight in *dukkha* is also developed in several Chinese discourses, whenever the four noble Truths are understood (MA 102 and the EA 'Discourse on the cultivation of recollection'). The EA *Ānāpāna-Sūtra* stresses the contemplation of impermanence, while the Pali MN 62 develops the insight that the elements of existence and the four elements are not the self.

The Pali and Chinese discourses on mindfulness of the breath SA 810 and MN 118 are parallels, which also lead to almost the same results or 'fruits'. We called six pairs of Pali and Chinese discourses partial parallels; however, for four of these the results differ. These four pairs which offer different 'fruits' are MA 10-MN 2, MA 93-MN 7, MA 14-MN 61, and EA *Ānāpāna-Sūtra*-MN 62. On the other hand we found the same results in MA 204-MN 26, and also in the MA redaction on the four foundations of mindfulness and MN 10. The Chinese *Discourse on the cultivation of recollection* of the EA and DN 22 are only related, but the 'fruits' show partial parallels.

Chapter 6

Summary and conclusions

Current methods of *vipassanā*-meditation (Chapter 2)

Teachers and scholars use several terms to describe *vipassanā*: insight, clear insight, deep insight, real knowledge and vision, understanding, seeing, intuitive insight, experiences and understands, realisation, see reality, insight knowledge, and liberating knowledge. These terms try to make clear that this insight or knowledge must be experienced and understood.

We are interested in the methods to reach *vipassanā*, and therefore we began with comparing the methods of *vipassanā*-meditation by the meditation teachers with those of the scholar-monks as discussed above.

Fifteen of the twenty-one teachers investigated based their methods on *sati* as explained in the discourses DN 22, MN 10, MN 118 or MN 119. Furthermore, *sutta* MN 62 which is relevant for the analysis of the four great elements also teaches attention to breathing. Three teachers apply analysis of the four great elements; this method may be based on MN 28 or MN 62.

Scholar monks more often mentioned MN 10 and a number of AN *sutta*s to explain the development of *sati*. The scholar-monks support the teachers, who base their methods of *vipassanā*-meditation on a form of *sati*-practice, but according to the scholar-monks it should not be the only practice. They teach that training in virtue and developing concentration to at least the first *jhāna* are necessary, except Nyanaponika who states that insight can be attained in access concentration.

Among the teachers there are only four who deem such *jhāna* concentration is needed, while nine believe that a lower level of concentration is sufficient or even better. The scholar-monks agree with many teachers that *vipassanā* means, or *vipassanā* practice develops, the insight that body and mind are impermanent, suffering and not the self.

Requirements of systematic training to develop insight (Chapter 3)

Besides training in virtue and development of concentration, *Vipassanā*-meditation requires perception of impermanence, of suffering, and of this is not my self. *Sutta*s MN 74 (I, 500), MN 148 and AN 5.72 (III, 85 f.) combine these perceptions with thorough development of the thoughts of renunciation and of dispassion resulting in liberation, or in mind emancipation and insight-emancipation.

The understanding of the four noble Truths equals the training in the higher insight (AN 3.88-I, 235), and the training in the higher insight destroys the taints (AN 3.89-I, 235 f.). MN 4 (I, 23) concurs that such understanding of the four noble Truths and of the taints leads to knowledge of release. The systematic training to develop insight towards wisdom should be called "*vipassanā-bhāvanā*", translated as development of insight in this research.

Some practices often included in the development of *vipassanā* lack a canonical foundation according to several scholar-monks. This applies to the development of the group of sixteen *ñāṇa*s which follows a Theravāda tradition, which is later than the *sutta*s. Dry insight, without the support of mental calm, is an idea found in the commentaries, and it is not traced in the early discourses either.

Our first working hypothesis, based on the methods of the twenty-one teachers discussed in Chapter 2, stated: 'Practices which only teach attention to the breath only teach one step of the eightfold Path, namely *sati*.' Indeed, according to most of the scholar-monks discussed above, morality and concentration to at least the first *jhāna* are necessary besides *sati*. However, just noting the breath trains tranquillity. According to MN 118, full development of attention to the breath can even lead to insight and freedom. Thus this *sutta* offers a method contrary to our first working hypothesis.

According to several *sutta*s such as DN 22 and MN 141, right concentration as part of the noble eightfold Path comprises the four *jhāna*s; other *sutta*s argue at least the first *jhāna* is necessary to win insight and destruction of the taints (MN 64-I, 435; AN 9.36-IV, 422). Furthermore, the level of tranquillity needed before beginning the development of insight has not been fixed (AN 4.170-II, 157). These findings are in agreement with the second working hypothesis:

> 'a) The level of concentration needed to reach clear insight has not been indicated in an unequivocal way in the *suttas*.' And b) 'the idea that momentary concentration is sufficient for release, is contrary to right concentration'

Insight into the impermanence of the five elements of existence or constituents of a 'person' features in many discourses as a last step to liberation by destroying the taints (DN 14-II, 35; DN 33-III, 223; SN 18.22-II, 253; AN 4.41-II, 44 ff., and AN 8.2-IV 153). This insight ends clinging to a self (SN 18.22-II, 253) or even ends clinging to anything (DN 14-II, 35).

However, alternatively the "liberating insight" may mean the understanding of the four noble Truths according to DN 22; MN 141 and AN 3.88 (I, 235), because this understanding implies full insight into the dependent arising of suffering (*dukkha*) and its ending. Training in the higher insight may also lead to destruction of the taints and release, according to AN 3.89 (I, 235 f.). In MN 4 the liberating knowledge comprises the understanding of the four noble Truths and of the taints. So, the content of the final insight, which is necessary according to many discourses, shows variations. These results corroborate the third working hypothesis: 'The final step to awakening remains uncertain.'

Pali discourses on training towards insight (Chapter 4)

Several principles related to insight (*vipassanā*) and its development are widely accepted in the Pali *suttas*. Impermanence, suffering, and this is not my self (*anicca, dukkha, anattā*) must be seen with insight, according to MN 22 (I, 138 f.), MN 74 and AN 7.46 (IV, 46). These are the so called characteristics or marks of existence. According to the method of MN 74 (I, 499 f.), such insight is based on considering that the body consists of four [great] elements and the impermanence of feelings. Seeing feelings in this way one gets enough of feelings, one becomes passionless and is freed. MN 148 teaches impermanence, not the self, and abandoning the tendencies to feelings, for arousing true knowledge. Seeing thus can lead towards the end of suffering by disenchantment with feeling and with craving, leading to dispassion, and finally to liberation from the taints.

The destruction of the taints (*āsavas*) of lust, [desire for] becoming, and ignorance accomplishes freedom through wisdom, see for instance MN 6-I, 35-6 and AN 3.89-I, 235).

The four states of right concentration (*jhānas*) are part of the process to develop wisdom, or even lead to the final insight according to for example DN 22 (II, 290 ff.) and MN 141 (III, 252). However, other discourses teach that in the first *jhāna* or in any higher concentration, liberation by insight may be reached by contemplation of *jhāna* (MN 52-I, 350; AN 11.17-V, 343).

Only a few *suttas* combine training in most of the elements directly related to insight, namely the characteristics of existence and the destruction of the taints, together with a sufficient level of concentration in a single teaching. The least complex approach to concentration and insight is to accept *suttas* which teach most aspects of it as methods to develop liberating insight or wisdom. So we suggest the following *suttas* may be most suitable for training purposes towards liberating insight, because specific practices thus remain in their context and less additional elements have to be taught:

By following DN 2 (I, 60 ff.) concentration and insight in the origin and destruction of the taints can be developed. Insight in impermanence (*anicca*) is lacking in DN 2. This may be trained with exercises taught in MN 118 (III, 83 f.), MN 146 (III, 270 ff.) or AN 7.46 (IV, 46 ff.).

Sutta DN 22 (II, 290 ff.) trains mindfulness and concentration. Contemplating the mental factors leads to understanding the four noble Truths, which includes full insight in suffering, and finally to liberating insight. In this discourse *anattā* and *anicca* are implicit in origination - dissolution of the body, as we cannot control this process. A combination of DN 22 with MN 62 offers an explicit method to understand this is not my self (*anattā*) and impermanence (*anicca*). It is remarkable that the taints of craving for becoming and of ignorance have not been mentioned in DN 22.

According to some *suttas* it is possible to contemplate impermanence, suffering, and this is not my self while in *jhāna*, leading to insight in these characteristics of existence (MN 64-I, 435 ff. and AN 9.36 V, 422 ff.). Then one concentrates on the sublime (*nibbāna*), which may destroy the taints (MN 64-I, 436 f.).

Sutta MN 118 teaches to observe the process of breathing. One trains to develop penetrative awareness of the impermanent nature of reality and to observe detachment, stopping and casting away (MN 118-III, 83 f.). These may be regarded as practices specifically aimed at insight. After developing an unspecified level of concentration, one develops equanimity as the final phase of the seven links for awakening. Full development of these links is sufficient for liberation.

However, MN 118 does not explicitly teach how to develop insight in *dukkha* and *anattā*. The method taught in MN 22 (I, 138) may complement these insights thus: seeing impermanence should lead on to insight into unsatisfactoriness and into this is not my self, as it is not appropriate to see what is impermanent, unsatisfactory and subject to change as "this is my self". This combination constitutes a method to become passionless without *jhāna* and results in liberating insight. The *Vinaya* (*Mahāvagga* I, 6.38-41-I, 13-14) teaches the same as MN 22, and that *Vinaya* text also states that one cannot control the elements of existence and so they are not self.

Sutta MN 4 explains the four *jhāna*s, leading to understanding of the four noble Truths and the taints. *Sutta* AN 3.88 (I, 235) calls the understanding of the four Truths the training in the higher insight, and according to AN 3.89 (I, 235 f.) this training destroys the taints.

Comparison of Chinese and Pali discourses relevant for insight and wisdom (Chapter 5)

We draw the following conclusions from the comparison of some Chinese *sūtra*s and related Pali discourses to find the relationship of insight, the taints, and liberation. Insight may be part of a process to develop freedom through wisdom (MA 211) or freedom through intuitive wisdom (MN 43). The relationship of wisdom with liberation is strong in Chinese discourses. The destruction of the same three taints as in many Pali *sutta*s and wisdom go together with liberation in several of these Chinese *sūtra*s (MA 81 and EA 11.20.7), and so support Pali discourses such as MN 2, MN 7, and MN 119.

However, we traced no support in the sources about the translations or in the references to Chinese discourses for a method that solely develops insight and destruction of the taints towards liberation, such as we found in the Pali discourses MN 22, MN 74 and MN 148.

Several methods leading to mindfulness are taught for developing knowledge in Chinese renderings. Calm or concentration has a role in these methods as taught in the EA "*Discourse on the cultivation of recollection*" where the training includes the four noble Truths or in SA 810 as part of the seven factors of awakening. Furthermore, in both EA 11.20.7 and AN 2.3.10 (I, 61) calm and insight are needed for liberation. On these points the Chinese *sūtra*s corroborate the Pali *sutta*s.

However, the insight in the three characteristics of existence (impermanence, suffering, and this is not the self) as a group is rarely part of the Chinese teachings discussed. Still, the relationship of seeing all three characteristics with the destruction of the taints and knowledge of emancipation is taught in MA 75. Insight in impermanence sometimes is part of the training in discourses on mindfulness. *Sūtra* MA 102 and the EA 'Discourse on the cultivation of recollection' develop insight in suffering by understanding the four noble Truths.

The concept "this is not the self" or "not mine" seems to be rare in the *Madhyama-Āgama*, thus differing from the Pali *suttas*. The *Ānāpāna-Sūtra* of the *Ekottara-Āgama* compared with *Majjhima-Nikāya sutta* 62 supports this difference in emphasis thus: this EA discourse gives much attention to the contemplation of impermanence, while the Pali MN 62 develops the insight that the constituents or the five elements of existence are not the self.

Conclusion

Insight has to be developed by training, not only in mindfulness, but also by developing concentration to attain at least the first *jhāna*. It seems better to call this "*vipassanā-bhāvanā*" or the development of insight than *vipassanā*-meditation, as different methods of training are needed. The characteristics of existence, namely impermanence, suffering, and this is not the self (*anicca, dukkha, anattā*), must be seen with insight according to many Pali *suttas*. However, the discourses in Chinese that were investigated in this study rarely include insight in the concept of "this is not the self".

The destruction of the taints (*āsavas*) of craving, of desire for becoming, and of ignorance, equals liberation according to several Pali and Chinese canonical texts.

We did not trace any Chinese corroboration for the Pali *suttas* (MN 22, MN 74, and MN 148) that offer a method to develop insight and destruction of the taints towards liberation without concentration to *jhāna*. For the systematic training in both concentration and *vipassanā* combinations of at least two *suttas* are needed.

References

Explanation of references to Pali discourses

References to discourses are to editions or translations of the Pali Text Society, unless otherwise indicated.

For the *Dīgha-Nikāya* (DN) and *Majjhima-Nikāya* (MN) the *sutta* number and then the group in Roman numbers and the page number of the edition are mentioned. Example: in the running text as DN 22 (II, 291) or at the end of a sentence as (DN 22-II, 291).

For the *Aṅguttara-Nikāya* (AN) books of ones and twos we use: book-, chapter-, paragraph-number of the *sutta,* and then volume and the page number of the edition; example: AN 2.17.3 (I, 100) or (AN 2.17.3-I, 100). For AN books 3 till 11, a more simple system could be used: book, number from the beginning of the book plus volume and page of the edition. Example: AN 4.94 (II, 92 f.) or (AN 4.94-II, 92 f.).

The *Saṃyutta-Nikāya* (SN), volumes one to four, is referred to by chapter and paragraph-number of the *sutta*, plus volume and page of the edition; example: SN 12.23-II, 30. However, in volume five of the SN the translator used a more complicated system we had to follow, to that we added again the volume and page of the PTS edition. Example: SN XLVII, III, V, ii (V, 184).

A. Primary sources

Abhidhammattha Sangaha: a comprehensive manual of Abhidhamma, Bhikkhu Bodhi (ed.), Kandy, 2010 (1993).

Aṅguttara-Nikāya, vols I and II ed. R. Morris; rev. A.K. Warder; vols III-V ed. E. Hardy; vol. VI, Mabel Hunt; rev. by C.A.F. Rhys Davids, London 1955-1961 (1885-1910) , 6 vols.

Aṅguttara-Nikāya, '*Gradual sayings*', vols I, II and V transl. F.L. Woodward; vols III and IV transl. E.M. Hare, London 1955-1960 (1932-6), 5 vols.

Aṅguttara-Nikāya, 'Numerical discourses of the Buddha: an anthology of suttas fom the Aṅguttara-Nikāya', transl. Nyanaponika and Bhikkhu Bodhi, Kandy 1999.

Dīgha-Nikāya, '*Thus have I heard: the long discourses of the Buddha'*, transl. M. Walshe, London, 1987.

Dīgha-Nikāya, *'De verzameling van lange leerredes'*, Dutch transl. J. de Breet and R. Janssen, Rotterdam 2001.

'The Discourse on the Foundations of Mindfulness' of the *Madhyama-Āgama*, transl. into Chinese in 397-398 CE by Gautama Samghadeva and in English by Bhikkhu Saddhaloka, in: *Buddhist Friendship*, Hongkong 1983, pp. 9-18.

Ekottara-Āgama, seventh fascicle, Part 17, *Ānāpāna [smṛti]-Sūtra,* transl. Thich Huyên-Vi and Bhikkhu Pāsādika, in: *Buddhist Studies Review* 10, 2 (1993), pp. 213-22.

Ekottara-Āgama, eleventh fascicle, Part 20 (T2, 599c5 ff.), *sutta* 7, transl. Thich Huyên-Vi and Bhikkhu Pāsādika, in: *Buddhist Studies Review* 18, 2 (2001), pp. 224-5.

Itivuttaka, transl. P. Masefield, Oxford 2000.

Majjhima-Nikāya, ed. V. Trenckner (vol. 1), London, 1964 (1888).

Majjhima-Nikāya, transl. I.B. Horner, 3 vols, London, 1954-9.

Majjhima-Nikāya, *'The middle length discourses of the Buddha: a translation of the Majjhima-Nikāya'*, transl. Bhikkhu Ñāṇamoli and Bhikkhu Bodhi, Boston 2009, 1995.

Majjhima-Nikāya, *'De verzameling van middellange leerredes'*, Dutch transl. J. De Breet and R. Janssen, Rotterdam 2004-5, 3 vols.

Milindapañho, *'De vragen van Milinda'*, Dutch transl. T. Kurpershoek-Scherft, Nieuwerkerk a/d IJssel 1998.

Paṭisambhidāmagga, *'The path of discrimination'*, transl. Bhikkhu Ñāṇamoli, London 1982.

Saṁyukta-Āgama, 'Mindfulness of breathing' (SA 810), transl. Anālayo, in: *Buddhist Studies Review* 24 (2), pp. 137-50.

Saṃyutta-Nikāya, *'Kindred sayings'*, vols I, II transl. Mrs. Rhys Davids; vols III-V transl. F.L. Woodward, 1950-1956 (1917-1930), London.

Saṃyutta-Nikāya, ed. L. Feer, London 1960 (1898).

'The *Smṛtyupasthānasūtra* of the *Ekottara-Āgama'*, translated from the Chinese version by Bhikkhu Pāsādika, in: *Facets of Indian Culture*, C.P. Sinha (ed.), Patna 1998, pp. 494-502.

Theragāthā, *'Elders' verses I'*, transl. K.R. Norman, London 1969.

Vimuttimagga, Arahant Upatissa, *'The path of freedom'*, translated from the Chinese version by the Rev. N.R.M. Elara, Soma Thera and Kheminda Thera, Colombo 1961.

Vinaya-Piṭaka, *Mahāvagga*, *'The book of discipline'*, vol. 4, transl. I.B. Horner, London 1962.

Visuddhimagga, Buddhaghosa, '*The path of* purification', transl. Ñāṇamoli, Berkeley etc. 1976.
Visuddhi-Magga, 'Der Weg zur Reinheit' transl. Nyanatiloka, Konstanz 1952.

B. Secondary sources

Access to Insight. Readings in Thervada Buddism, http://www.accesstoinsight.org
Achaan Naeb 1977, 'The development of insight', in: J. Kornfield (ed.), *Living Buddhist masters*, Santa Cruz.
Ajahn Chah 1982, *Bodhinyāna: a collection of Dhamma talks*, Ubon Rajathani.
Anālayo 2003, *Satipaṭṭhāna: the direct path to realization*, Birmingham.
– 2007 Mindfulness of breathing in the *Saṁyukta-Āgama*, in: *Buddhist Studies Review* 24 (2), pp. 137-50.
– 2008, *Reflections on Comparative Agama Studies*, in: *Chung-Hwa Buddhist Journal* 21, pp. 3-21, Taipei. E-link accessed 22.10.2011: http://www.buddhismuskunde.uni-hamburg.de/fileadmin/pdf/analayo/ReflectCompAgama.pdf
– 2010, *From grasping to emptiness,* New York.
– 2011, '*Purification, ethics and karma in the early Buddhist discourse*', lecture 6. E-link accessed 22. 10. 2011: http://www.buddhismuskunde.uni-hamburg.de/fileadmin/pdf/analayo/ lectures.htm
Bannaruji, B. (ed.) ca. 2006, *The five meditation techniques of Thai Buddhism*, Bangkok.
Bhikkhu Bodhi 1999, 'Introduction' in *Numerical discourses of the Buddha: an anthology of suttas from the Aṅguttara-Nikāya*, transl. Nyanaponika and Bhikkhu Bodhi, Kandy.
– 2009, *Majjhima-Nikāya, 'The middle length discourses of the Buddha: a translation of the Majjhima-Nikāya',* transl. Bhikkhu Ñāṇamoli and Bhikkhu Bodhi, Boston 2009 (1995).
Cousins, L.S. 1996, 'The origins of insight meditation', in: *The Buddhist Forum 4*, Skorupski, T. ed., London 2004 (1996), pp. 35-57.
Dhiravamsa, V.R. 1979, *Angenommen Sie fühlen sich Elend.*

– 1990, *Turning to the source: an Eastern view of Western mind using insight meditation and psychotherapy for personal growth, health & wholeness*, Nevada City.

Goenka, S.N. 1995 (1987), *The discourse summaries*, Igatpuri.

Gombrich, R.F. 1983, 'From monastery to meditation centre: lay meditation in modern Sri Lanka', in: *Buddhist studies: ancient and modern*, P. Denwood and A. Piatigorsky (eds.), London etc.

– 1988, *Theravāda Buddhism: a social history from ancient Benares to modern Colombo*, London etc.

– 1996, How Buddhism began: the conditioned genesis of the early teachings, London etc.

Gunaratana, H. 2008 (2002), *Meditatie in alle eenvoud*, Haarlem.

Hart, W. 1987, *The art of living: as taught by S.N. Goenka*, transl. in Dutch W. Suk and H. Wanningen, Amsterdam 2004.

Hinüber, O. von 2001 (1996), *A handbook of Pāli literature*, New Delhi.

Houtman, G. 1999, *Mental culture in Burmese crisis politics: Aung San Su Kyi and the national league for democracy*, Tokyo.

Jordt, I. 2007, *Burma's mass lay meditation movement: Buddhism and the cultural construction of power*, Athens (USA).

Kornfield, J. (ed.) 1977, *Living Buddhist masters*, Santa Cruz.

Kurpershoek-Scherft, T. 1998, '*De vragen van Milinda: een samenspraak tussen een Griekse koning en een boeddhistische monnik*', Nieuwerkerk a/d IJssel.

Ledi Sayādaw 1986 (1915), *The Manual of insight: Vipassanā Dīpanī,* transl. U Nyāna, Kandy.

Lexikon des Buddhismus, F.-K. Ehrhard, I.F. Fisher-Schreiber; S. Schumacher, G. Woerner (eds.), 1992, Bern etc.

Macqueen, G. 1988, *A study of the Śrāmaṇyaphala-sūtra*, Wiesbaden.

Mahāsi Sayādaw 1977, 'Insight meditation', in: J. Kornfield (ed.), *Living Buddhist masters*, Santa Cruz.

– 1989 (1979), *Instructies tot de Wipassanā: inzichtmeditatie*, Dutch translation by Dhammawīranātha 1979, Den Haag.

Mettavīhari, K.K. 1987, *The sixteen ñāṇas*, Amsterdam.

– 1989, *Vipassanā-meditation: und ihre Kenntnis*, Utrecht.

Norman, K.R. 1989 (1971), 'Elders' verses II' in: *Poems of early Buddhist Nuns*, Oxford.

Nyanaponika Thera 1975 (1962), *The heart of Buddhist meditation: a handbook of mental training based on the Buddha's way of mindfulness*, London.

Pali-English Dictionary, T.W. Rhys Davids and W. Stede (eds.), PTS, London 1999 (1921).

Pāli Tipiṭakaṁ concordance, F.L. Woodward and E.M. Hare (eds.), London, 1956, vol.1.

Salzberg, S., www.sharonsalzberg.com , accessed 05.12.2011.

Schmithausen, L. 1981, 'On some aspects of descriptions or theories of 'liberating insight' and 'enlightenment' in early Buddhism', in: *Studien zum Jainismus und Buddhismus: Gedenkschrift für Ludwig Alsdorf*, Wiesbaden.

Shankman, R. 2008, '*The experience of samādhi: an in depth exploration of Buddhist meditation*', Boston, London.

Sharf, R.H. 1995, 'Buddhist modernism and the rhetoric of meditative experience', in: *Numen*, Vol. 42, pp. 228-276.

Soma Thera 1961, 'Contemplation in the Dhamma', Appendix to the *Vimuttimagga*, Colombo. Originally published in: *Bosat*, July 1959.

Sujato 2001, *A swift pair of messengers,* PDF file.

– 2010 (rev.ed.), *A swift pair of messengers,* (e-book: www.santifm.org/santipada/2010/aswiftpairofmessengers).

– 2012 (2005) *A History of Mindfulness: How insight worsted tranquillity in the Satipaṭṭhāna Sutta*, (e-book: http://santipada.org, accessed 01.07.2013).

Thanissaro Bhikkhu, AN 9.44 (IV, 452 f.) in www.accesstoinsight.org, accessed 04.07.2010.

Thich Minh Chau (ca.) 1964, *The Chinese Madhyama-Āgama and the Pāli Majjhima-Nikāya: a comparative study*, Saigon.

Tse-fu Kuan 2008 (e-book 2007), *Mindfulness in early Buddhism*, London and New York.

Tullius, F. (ed.) 1988, *Vipassana Bhavana*: *theory practice and result*, Pattaya.

Vetter, T. 1988, '*The ideas and meditative practices of early Buddhism*', Leiden etc.

– 2000, *The 'khandha passages' in the Vinayapiṭaka and the four main Nikāyas*, Wien.

Abbreviations

AN	*Aṅguttara-Nikāya*
BSR	*Buddhist Studies Review*
ca.	circa
Dhp	*Dhammapāda*
DN	*Dīgha-Nikāya*
EA	Chinese *Ekottara-Āgama*
ed.	Edition
(ed.)	Editor
f.	and following page
ff.	and following pages
It	*Itivuttaka*
lit.	literal
MA	Chinese *Madhyama-Āgama*
MN	*Majjhima-Nikāya*
N and B	Nyanaponika and Bhikkhu Bodhi
Patis	*Paṭisambhidāmagga*
PTS	Pali Text Society
SA	Chinese *Saṁyukta-Āgama*
SN	*Saṃyutta-Nikāya*
Th	Theragāthā
transl.	translation
Tse	Case Tsê, Hsü-ts'ang, Japanese edition
Ud	*Udāna*
Vin	*Vinaya*
Vis	*Visuddhimagga*
vol.	volume
vols	volumes

Glossary of Pali and Sanskrit terms

The terms are in Pali, unless Sanskrit is indicated.

adhipaññādhamma-vipassanāya	wisdom of the higher and insight into *Dhamma*.
adhi-paññāsikkhā	training in the higher insight.
Āgama	collections of canonical texts of old Buddhist schools [Sanskrit or Chinese].
ānāpānasati	mindfulness of in- and out breathing.
anattā	this is not my self, 'non-self', no abiding individual entity.
anupassana	constant observation.
anattānupassana	seeing there is no individual entity.
anicca	impermanent, impermanence.
aniccānupassana	contemplation of impermanence [of *nāma* and *rūpa*].
aññā	profound knowledge.
anupassanā	contemplation.
Arahat, Arahant, Arhat	A worthy one, 'Saint', one who has attained perfection.
Arahatta	the state of being an *Arahat.*
Āranyaka	[a monk] who lives in the forest.
ārupa	[concentration on the] formless.
*arūpajhāna*s	formless concentrations.
*āsava*s	'fluxes' (lit.), taints, cankers, imperfections, corruptions:
kāmāsava	the taint of sensual craving, sense-desire;
bhavāsava	the taint of desire for continued existence, for becoming;
avijjāsava	the taint of ignorance.
asekha	'beyond training', often meaning an *Arahat.*
ātman (Sanskrit)	the Self, the soul.
ātmagraha (Sanskrit)	belief in a Self.
avaśyskārya (Sanskrit)	what has necessarily to be done.
avidyā (Sanskrit)	ignorance.
avijjā	ignorance.

*bhāṇaka*s	reciters of a group of discourses.
bhava	becoming.
bhāvanā	mental cultivation, systematic training, development.
bhāvetabbā	have to be cultivated.
*bhikkhu*s	monks.
bhikṣu (Sanskrit)	monk.
bodhāya	wisdom that is awakening.
brahmacarya	the holy life.
*brahmavihāra*s	'divine abodes', 'immeasurables', meditation exercises on loving kindness etc.
citta	[state of] mind etc.
*deva*s	gods.
Dhamma	the Buddhist doctrine.
Dhammakaya-Gotrabhu	a noble state.
*dhamma*s	things, phenomena, everything that exists.
dukkha	unsatisfactoriness, suffering, etc.
Duhkhanirodha (Sanskrit)	final cessation of suffering.
dukkhānupassana	contemplation of unsatisfactoriness.
dukkha-sacca	the noble Truth of suffering.
dhyāna (Sanskrit)	meditative absorption.
jhāna	meditative absorption of the mind, one of four states of right concentration.
kalāpa	small particle.
kāmāsrava (Sanskrit)	sensual craving, desire.
kamma	action.
kanika samādhi	momentary concentration.
kāya	body, may be also: the whole breath.
kasiṇa	device for concentration.
aloka kasiṇa	device for concentration on light.
kilesa	defilement, stain, obstacle, unwholesome root:
lobha	greed;
dohsa	anger;
moha	bewilderment.
*khandha*s	the five elements of existence of an 'individual', aggregates, constituents.
kṣaya (Sanskrit)	destruction.

mada (Sanskrit)	arrogance.
magga	the [Buddhist] way, paths of emancipation.
magga-ñāṇa	knowledge of the [Buddhist] way.
māna (Sanskrit)	conceit.
ñāṇa	knowledge.
nāma-rūpa	name and body (lit.), mental processes and material factors of an 'individual'.
Nibbāna	the goal of the Pali Buddhist doctrine: the end of suffering; extinction of desire, hatred, and ignorance.
Nikāya	group or collection [of discourses] of the Pali canon.
Nirvāṇa (Sanskrit)	extinction of desire, hatred, and ignorance.
Nivarāna	five hindrances.
pajānāti	he or she knows.
paññā	wisdom, discernment, liberating, knowledge.
paññindriyam	the faculty of insight.
paññāvimutti	liberation by wisdom, released through discernment.
phassa	contact, stimulus, sense-impression.
patipadā-ñāṇadassana-visudhi	purity of insight-knowledge of the Path.
phala-ñāṇa	knowledge of the fruit, result.
pīti	joy.
rūpa	'body'.
sacca	true, truth.
Sacca Dhamma	the true doctrine.
samādhi	deep concentration of the mind.
samatha	tranquillity, calmness, serenity.
samathi	steadiness of mind.
sammā-diṭṭhi	right understanding.
sammā-ñāṇam	right knowledge.
sammā-samādhi	right concentration, the four *jhāna*s.
sammā-vimutti	right liberation.
sampajañña	clear comprehension.
samudaya-sacca	truth of the origin [of suffering].
saṁyojana	fetters, (defilements).

saṅkhārā	mental reactions to liking and disliking.
saṇyojana	fetters, binds.
sati	mindfulness, awareness, intentness of mind, alertness, attention to here and now; (lit.) memory, recollection.
satipaṭṭhānas	the foundations of mindfulness.
śikṣāpada (Sanskrit)	rules of moral training.
sīla	moral practice, Buddhist ethics.
sotāpatti-magga	stream-entry.
sukha	pleasant, happiness.
sūtra (Sanskrit)	discourse, teaching.
sutta	discourse, teaching.
Sutta-Piṭaka	the basket of the Teaching.
taṇhā	craving
Theravāda	the Teaching of the Elders; the Buddhist tradition in Southeast-Asia.
upacāra-samādhi	access concentration.
upekkhā-sati-pārisuddhi	a state of pure equanimity and mindfulness.
vimukti (Sanskrit)	liberation, freedom.
vimutti	liberation, freedom.
vijjā	gnosis, knowledge.
Vinaya	[canonical texts on mainly] monastic discipline.
vipaśyana (Sanskrit)	penetrating insight.
vipassanā	Insight, [penetrating] insight, intuition and introspection etc.
vipassanā-bhāvanā	Insight-practice, insight-meditation.

Terms as used in the text, with additions based on:
Nyanaponika Thera 1975 (1962), *The heart of Buddhist meditation*; *Pali-English Dictionary,* T.W. Rhys Davids and W. Stede (eds.), PTS, 1999 (1921); *Lexikon des Buddhismus*, 1992.

Index of teachers and scholar-monks discussed, by section